Financially Fit

How to manage your money, get out of debt, build wealth, and *enjoy the ride!*

A Three-Part Series

Book 3: Your Path to Financial Freedom

By

Dr. Tony Pennells M.B.B.S, Dip. FS

By the Author

Dr. Tony Pennells M.B.B.S, Dip. FS

☙

Books

Financially Fit - Book One: How to Cure Money Stress

Financially Fit - Book Two: 30 Days to Financial Fitness

Financially Fit - Book Three: Your Path to Financial Freedom

Connect with me!

I love getting feedback from my readers and would really appreciate you taking a few minutes to post your comments or a brief review on my Amazon page.

https://www.amazon.com/author/drtonypennells

Also come join our Facebook community here:

Facebook - www.facebook.com/finfitwithdrtony

Thank you!

Disclaimer

General Advice Disclaimer

This book is presented solely for educational and general information regarding the subject matter covered. The author and publisher are not offering it as financial, legal, accounting, or other professional services advice. Whilst reasonable precautions have been taken to ensure the accuracy of the material contained herein at the time of publication, no person, persons or organisation should invest monies or take action on reliance of the material contained herein but instead should satisfy themselves independently of the appropriateness of such action.

No Warranties

While reasonable precautions have been used in preparing this book, the author and publisher make no representations or warranties of any kind and assume no liabilities of any kind with respect to the accuracy or completeness of the contents and specifically disclaim any implied warranties of merchantability or fitness of use for a particular purpose. Neither the author nor the publisher shall be held liable or responsible to any person or entity with respect to any loss or incidental or consequential damages caused, or alleged to have been caused, directly or indirectly, by the information or programs contained herein. No warranty may be created or extended by sales representatives or written sales materials. Every person is different and the advice and strategies contained herein may not be suitable for your situation. You should seek the services of a competent professional before beginning any improvement program. Some parts of the story and its characters and entities may be fictional. Any likeness to actual persons, either living or dead, is strictly coincidental.

Liability Disclaimer

The publishers, authors, and any other parties involved in the creation, production, provision of information, or delivery of this book specifically disclaim any responsibility, and shall not be liable for any damages, claims, injuries, losses, liabilities, costs or obligations including any direct, indirect, special, incidental, or consequential damages (collectively known as "Damages") whatsoever and howsoever caused, arising out of, or in connection with, the use or misuse of the book and the information contained within it, whether such Damages arise in contract, tort, negligence, equity, statute law, or by way of any other legal theory.

You may *NOT* give away, share or resell this intellectual property in any way.

Copyright © 2013 by Dr Tony Pennells

All rights reserved. No part of this publication may be reproduced or transmitted in any form or by any means, electronic, or mechanical, including photocopying, recording, or by any information storage and retrieval system, without written permission from the publisher.

Published by: Doncarie Pty Ltd

Dedication

I dedicate this book to you.

May the knowledge that I share help to permanently remove Money Stress from your life, and lead you on a path filled with fun, freedom and adventure!

Table of Content

Introduction 1

Part One What is your Dream? 5

Chapter 1 What's your dream? 6

Chapter 2 The 4 Stages of Financial Health 12

Chapter 3 What does Financial Freedom actually look like? 17

Part Two Your Path to Financial Freedom 26

Stage One Becoming *Financially Fit* 27

Chapter 4 What you need to know 28

Chapter 5 What you need to do 39

Chapter 6 Graduating Stage One 74

Stage Two Moving up to being *Financially Secure* 77

Chapter 7 What you need to know 78

Chapter 8 What you need to do 89

Chapter 9 Graduating to the next stage 117

Stage Three Path to *Financially Independence* 120

Chapter 10 What you need to know 121

Chapter 11 What you need to do 129

Chapter 12 Graduating to the next stage 142

Stage Four Your Journey to *Financial Freedom* and Beyond 146

Chapter 13 What you need to know 147

Chapter 14 What you need to do 164

Chapter 15 Graduating to the next stage 184

Promises 190

Epilogue 199

Research 205

Connect with me! 208

Introduction

Welcome to Financially Fit.

This is the third book in the *Financially Fit* series. The previous two books were written to lay the foundation for getting you to this point.

In the first book – *How to Cure Money Stress* - we looked at the money mistakes that you must avoid if you wish to have any chance of becoming financially fit, and ultimately financially free.

In the second book – *"30 days to Financial Fitness"* - we discussed the four pillars of wealth. These are the four key principles that underlie any successful journey towards financial freedom.

In this book we get down into the specifics. This is where the rubber hits the road!

While it can certainly be read as a stand-alone, you will be at an advantage if you have read the first to book before jumping into this one.

Here we will be building on the principles from the first books, and tying it all together into a step-by-step plan. The goal is nothing less than for you to have a clear path to follow that will take you to *Financial Independence* and on to *Financial Freedom*.

What can you expect to get out of this book?

I've broken this book up into several parts.

We begin with getting a clear picture of what it is that you are building.

I repeat - the goal for you is to achieve nothing less than true financial freedom. But what does that actually look like?

Has anyone ever shown you exactly what *Financial Freedom* really looks like?

Well in part one I'm going to show you.

It is vital that you can clearly see what it is you are trying to achieve. Having a clear picture in your mind exponentially increases your chance of success.

In the second part, I'll be showing you exactly how you build your financial dream by graduating through each of the four stages of Financial Health.

I will be covering such things as:

- exactly where your savings should go
- how to structure your bank accounts so that they work for you
- whether you should get out of debt, or build wealth first
- how to terminate your debts with extreme prejudice
- what you should be investing in, and
- how to build wealth and achieve freedom.

By the end of this book you should be able to see a clear path from where you are today through to your dream lifestyle.

You will also be able to convert it into a step-by-step financial plan (and know exactly where you need to start today).

I don't promise that it will be easy. Like any fitness plan you should expect some degree of discomfort and discipline until the workouts become a habit.

What I do promise though is that the plan will be simple, and it works!

I have had the absolute pleasure of helping people turn their financial lives around by taking these *exact same steps* that I will be working through with you in this book.

If you are prepared to pay the price of discipline to put the plan into action for yourself, you will definitely start to become financially fitter and stronger within a matter of days.

Let's begin.

Part One

What is your Dream?

Chapter 1

What's your dream?

"Can you see your dream? The clearer your goal, the easier it is for your mind to see the path you must take to reach it." Dr. Tony Pennells

What do you actually want?

You need to be specific.

Most people that I talk to tell me that they want to "get ahead" financially. I usually ask them what they mean by that. Almost always I get a version of the following non-specific answers:

"I want to be able to not worry about money."
"I don't want to have to work all my life."
"I want to be financially successful."

"I want a better life."
"I want to be able to spend without worrying about money."
You get the idea…

When I then ask "So where do you need to be financially for that to become a reality?", most people have no clear picture of what their desire or dream <u>actually</u> looks like.

Let me give you a big success tip – if you cannot clearly see or describe what your goal is, you almost certainly will not be able to achieve it.

Begin with the End in Mind

Let's now take the time to get a clear picture of the life you want to build.

It is very important that you are as specific as possible. If your mind can grasp a clear picture it will move you steadily towards it, but it cannot handle vague or changing wishes.

In the first book, *How to Cure Money Stress,* I spoke about the game of money. The object of the game is to get your 'dam' of investments to be large enough to give you the choice not to have to work for money.

The point at which this first becomes possible is the point at which you become *Financially Independent* – or graduate through the end of the third stage of Financial Health.

This is the exact point at which your life starts to change significantly. You now can have your time back if you wish. You can choose to no longer have to answer to a boss or a job. You become the master of your own destiny. This is the exact point I would like you to focus on.

Remember that I'm not talking about you living a life of the 'rich and famous' at this stage - that can come later. What I am talking about is you reaching the point of being truly financially independent – i.e. being able to support your current lifestyle (maybe with a few changes) through your investments.

I'd like you to concentrate on exactly how this picture looks. Close your eyes and imagine yourself within this picture like you have already accomplished it. Now answer these questions:

How does your life look?
How old are you?
What house are you living in?
What country or city are you living in?
What type of work are you doing? (If any) How are you spending your time?

If you have children, are they still living with you, or are they now financially independent?

Do you have any debts? (The answer should be no, with the exception, perhaps, of some intelligent investment debt.)

When you are shopping, what are you spending your money on?

How often are you eating out, or going out for entertainment?

How often, and where, are you going on holiday each year?

Can you see it? How clear does the picture look in your mind?

Now take the time to write this down either on the lines below to begin with, or onto a new document or clean piece of paper.

_____
_____
_____
_____
_____
_____
_____
_____
_____
_____
_____

Now for the key step in being able to start converting this picture into a financial plan.

How much investment income do you need each month to live the life that you see in your picture?

_____

Is it $4000 a month, $5000 a month, $7000 a month, $10,000 a month, etc?

Remember that at this first point of becoming financially independent you are probably debt free, and may no longer have any large expenses for any children you may have. So there is a very good chance that you actually need significantly <u>less</u> income to maintain your lifestyle when you no longer have large monthly loan repayments, and are no longer supporting your kids financially.

Do you have the income number written down?

Good. Now I suggest that you write this goal down on a new piece of paper. I also find it helpful to find some pictures that relate to this goal and stick them onto the piece of paper as well. Now put this somewhere prominent, and look at it frequently to remind yourself of what you are working towards.

I was taught to do this a long time ago. In times when self-doubt or discouragement creeps in, as it most certainly will, you can pull the picture out and get the vision clear in your head again. Once you've reminded yourself how important the goal is to you, you can patch up your bruises, raise your head and take another step forward.

Remember that success comes every time that you are prepared to get up one more time than you fall.

Once you have a clear picture of your goal, your job is to now steadily work your way through each of the stages of Financial Health until you have reached *Financial Freedom*.

Chapter 2
The 4 Stages of Financial Health

"Do you want some simple but extremely rare advice? Here it is: If you want to get rich, focus on making, keeping, and investing your money. If you want to be poor, focus on spending your money. You can read a thousand books and take a hundred courses on success, but it all boils down to that. Remember, what you focus on expands." ~ T. Harv Eker, Secrets of the Millionaire Mind

~

In Book Two, *30 Days to Financial Fitness*, I discussed the 4 Pillars of Wealth in some detail. These are the following four principles that the wealthy universally follow:

1. Paying yourself first
2. Living within your means
3. Reinvesting your investment returns

4. Protecting yourself

I also briefly introduced the four stages of Financial Health. They are:

Stage One – Financially Fit
Stage Two – Financially Secure
Stage Three – Financially Independent
Stage Four – Financially Free

The aim of any long term wealth or financial plan is to ultimately be at least financially independent. In my experience, the only certain way to get there is by setting and working a plan to steadily graduate through Stages One, Two and Three in sequence. If you follow this plan, given enough time, you will almost certainly become at least financial independent.

Let me briefly cover how the principles and the Stages of Financial Health relate to each other.

Stage One: Financially Fit

It all starts with *financial fitness*. This is the foundation of the first of the money habits that makes the rest of the stages possible. The key principles at work in becoming *Financially Fit* are:

Rule 1 - Paying yourself first

Rule 2 - Living within your means

Mastering these two principles is the key to moving from Stage One to Stage Two.

With focus and commitment, the plan should be fully in place within 30 days, and the new habits learned within 90 days.

The key mistake that people can make is not to give this step the focus it deserves. It looks simple and pretty basic, but it is the most powerful and important step, and is absolutely critical to get right if you seriously wish to become financially successful.

Stage Two: Financially Secure

The focus of becoming *Financially Secure* is to build a safety net under you and your family. It is the first focus of what takes priority with the surplus cash you create from Stage One. The key principle at work in becoming *Financially Secure* is:

Rule 4 - Protecting yourself.

At this stage the focus is to have an emergency fund being built, begin terminating your debts, and having the right amount and the right type of personal insurances in place to cover any gaps in your personal safety net. This stage should be able to be well underway within 90 to 180 days of starting your Financial Freedom plan.

Stage Three: Financially Independent

If Stages One and Two were causes for celebration can you imagine the party when you reach Stage Three?

Financial independence occurs when you have enough investments to be able to last you until at least age 90. The key principle at work here is:

Rule 3 - Reinvesting your investment returns.

Obviously the better that you have done in Stages One and Two, the faster you are able to lock away becoming *Financially Independent*.

Stage Four: Financially Free

You become *Financially Free* when your investments are earning enough money for you to live off and pay all your bills.

This is the key stage to be planning for.

Once you have achieved this stage, the sky is then the limit. You will have the time, income and knowledge to increase your wealth as far as you wish. You don't need to be a movie star or rare genius to accomplish this, but you do need a plan.

That is what the remainder of this book is about.

Chapter 3

What does Financial Freedom actually look like?

So what does financial independence and financial freedom actually look like? Has anyone ever shown you?

Have you ever read a book, or been to a seminar where an 'expert' has spoken about financial freedom of financial independence? If you reading this book I'm sure you have. Did you find that what they spoke about was more of a concept, and they never really got down to the specifics of exactly what it looked like.

I was 22 years of age when I first saw the idea that financial independence was something that I could strive to achieve before I was 65 years of age. I still remember how slow my mind was to try to understand this concept for the first time. Up until then I thought that being financially successful meant working in a high paid profession. At that stage I was five years into a six-year medical degree. I paid to attend a workshop called 'Mind Mastery'. They were promoting, amongst other things, that they could teach you how to have a better memory – something that appealed to me given the vast amount of study that I was doing in medicine. This workshop gave me more than that. I walked away with an understanding and belief that human beings are capable of the most extraordinary feats, and that if we harnessed the power of choice, then we can design our own life.

For the first time I also understood that I didn't have to work for a living all of my life. Many people before me had learnt how to build investments and businesses that could run or work without them, and once they had done this they were free to spend their time as they chose.

This was without a doubt one of the most profound, and at the same time, most frustrating insights that I've ever experienced. Let me try to explain, and see if you can relate to me. At that moment I had a clear picture in my head of what my life would look like if I was financially free. I also knew that if someone had done it before me then there was no reason that I couldn't do it as well. All I needed to do was learn what they had done and copy it.

Little did I know how hard it would be to find out <u>exactly</u> what people had done in the journey to become truly financially free. I ended up spending many years, read dozens of books, spent well over one hundred thousand dollars attending countless seminars and workshops, and bought many successful people lunches and dinners so that I could 'pick their brains' and learn from their experiences and wisdom. Step-by-step I was slowly able to put together a clear picture of what true financial freedom looks like.

There are three key parts to having a clear understanding of financial freedom:

1. Knowing how much you need invested to be financially free.
2. Knowing what you should invest in, and how it should be structured.
3. Having a specific plan in place to take you from where you are now through to financial freedom within the timeframe you have set.

Let me share the first part with you now. I will be dealing with parts two and three in the second part of this book.

How much do you need to be financially independent?

In this section we going to take a look at how much you need to have invested and working for you to be *Financially Independent* or *Financially Free*.

Being *Financially Independent* is the end goal of the third stage of Financial Health. Being *Financially Free* is the end goal of the fourth stage of Financial Health.

So what's the difference?

Basically to be able to consider yourself *Financially Independent* you would need to have enough investments to last you for a minimum of 25 years of retirement (assume that this is from 65 years of age until you are 90 years old).

90 is the recommended minimum age that you should aim for to try to reduce the chance that your money runs out before you die. Yes, this is exactly as it sounds. The income from your assets is not enough to live off. You will need to also be selling your assets as you go along to give you enough money to live off each month.

It is basically a game of Russian roulette with the aim to hope that your money lasts as long as you do.

This is how almost all financial planners work when they put a retirement plan in place for you.

Financial Independence is the minimum level to aim for, and once it has been secured you continue to shoot for true *Financial Freedom*.

To consider yourself to be *Financially Free* you would need to have your invested assets making enough <u>income</u> for you to live off without ever having to sell the actual assets.

Let's take a look at how much you would need to have invested to be firstly *Financially Independent*, and then to be *Financially Free*:

<u>Stage Three: Financially Independent</u>
How much do you need to be financially independent?

The answer to this question depends on two things:

- How much money you need to live on each year; and
- How many years you need the money to last for.

The simplest way to calculate how much money you will need to be financially independent is to multiply how much money you need each year by how many years you need the money to last for. (I know some people will say but I haven't allowed for the income your money will be earning at this stage, but to keep it simple I'll assume that it is invested very conservatively, and the amount of money it earns is just enough to keep up with the rising cost of living or inflation.)

Let's say for example, that you want to be financially independent by age 65. By that age you plan to be debt free, and the kids are off your hands, so you feel you could get by on $40,000 a year. You want your money to last at least 25 years until age 90.

In this example you will need:

Amount of $ each year x Number of years
$40,000 x 25years = $1,000,000

So in this example you will need to aim for $1 million of investments (in today's money value) to consider yourself to be financially independent by age 65.

Stage Four: Financial Freedom
This is definitely the stage you want to be aiming for.

It is not that much past Stage Three if you start early enough and are focused.

Here you don't have to worry about your money running out. Your money gets sent out to work, it earns its wage (whether that's interest, rent, dividends, or profit), and then goes straight back out to work again. And the best part is that once you no longer need it, you can pass your money onto your kids, and it go straight out to work for them.

How much do you need to be financially free?

The answer to this question also depends on two things. You will notice that the second point is different to Stage Three:

- How much money you need to live on each year; and
- What percentage investment return (or yield) you can have your money earning for you.

The simplest way to calculate how much money you need to be financially free is to divide how much money you need each year by the percentage investment return. (If you're not sure what percent investment return, I would suggest you use around 3% to give you an idea of what you are aiming for. This is very conservative – in many investments you should be able to get more than this, but you need to make sure that your investments continue to grow in value at least at the rate of inflation *after* you have taken your income out of it.)

Let's use the same example that we used for Stage Three previously. You want to have an income of $40,000 a year, and can have your money earning income at a yield of 3%.

In this example you will need:
Amount of $ each year *divided by* Investment Return (yield)
$40,000 / 3% = $1,333,333

Can you actually achieve that?

When you look at the above examples there are two things that I would like you to notice.

The first is that going for *Financial Freedom* is not that much further down the road than going for *Financial Independence*. So why not shoot for the stars? Go for *Freedom*. If you miss you should comfortably hit *Independence*.

Second is that achieving *Financial Freedom* or *Financial Independence* are not small goals. They require focus, commitment, and a specific plan to follow. What I can tell you is that the goals are absolutely achievable if you are prepared to pay the price.

The Financially Fit system that I will be sharing with you in Part Two of this book is the summary of all that I have learned over the past 20 years. I have broken it down, and simplified it into a step-by-step process that anyone can follow if they are prepared to put in some time and effort.

For the remainder of this book we will be putting the 'how-to' details into a plan of action that will become *Your Path to Financial Freedom*.

Part Two

Your Path to Financial Freedom

Stage One

Becoming *Financially Fit*

Chapter 4

What you need to know

What's the goal of Stage One?

Stage One is all about actually applying the first two principles within your life: Principle One - Pay Yourself First and Principle Two: Live Within Your Means.

As I've previously mentioned, this is the cornerstone of becoming wealthy.

If you fail to master this step, the chance of *ever* becoming financially independent dramatically reduces.

If you do master this step however, you will begin to find that step-by-step you become financially more secure, AND that the speed begins to accelerate in an exponential fashion.

With that in mind, I strongly suggest that you take the time to be sure that you follow these steps to the best of your ability.

Get in control

One of the key personal insights to successfully achieving this stage is to become comfortable that your money management is under control.

Pay yourself first

The next insight is the understanding that what you earn today is not only for your use today, but that it is absolutely imperative that a portion of it is automatically put away to look after you in the future.

Live within your means

With these to core beliefs in place, you will realize that you need to live within your means after paying yourself first. This will also be a way of ensuring this is not a sacrifice that will make your life any less enjoyable, but often in fact quite the opposite.

You are in complete control of all the decisions – it is just that now you are more proactive about prioritizing what you spend your money on.

Now it is about having a system in place that can work automatically, and is actually simple to stick to once it is in place. This will allow you to <u>automatically</u> get the rest of your life in order to make 'paying yourself first' happen

Needs vs. Wants

In Book Two we discussed needs versus wants in quite a bit of details. I'd like to take the time to refresh and recap understanding of what is truly a need and what is really a want.

You will always have desires greater than your ability to earn. This is human nature. Any person or group will always try to spend more than it makes.

This might not now seem realistic, but many of us could happily live on less than we are spending at the moment.

Think about it.

Most of us have been working for more than a couple of years and chances are that you are earning more today than what you were earning just three to five years ago, yet it still feels like we never quite have enough money.

You might remember the story of my friend Kate – a single mom working hard to raise two teenage daughters.

Kate argued with me that she was being very careful with her money, with almost every dollar being spent on needs, and not wants.

When we actually had a close look at where her money was going we found that she could free up a little more than $1,000 per month by prioritising her spending (yes…she couldn't believe that she was wasting more than $1,000 a month on wants).

With relatively small changes, she could get solidly on the path to Financial Health with minimal impact to her quality of life today – It was all about just taking control and prioritising where her money was going, and then setting some self-imposed limits.

Achieving wealth is usually not because we don't have enough money.

In fact, there are probably many people in your suburb that get by just fine earning quite a lot less than you. The basic problem is that we are not following the correct plan.

Often we confuse what we need to sustain basic living with wants.

A want is anything above the basics of what we need to get by.

For example:

- A nicer home than we need
- Buying new furniture, as well as any decorative items for the house
- Driving a nicer car than we need
- Private schooling
- Pay television
- Regular dining out - in fact probably *all* dining out
- Holiday spending
- Internet gaming subscriptions
- Most memberships
- Magazine subscriptions
- And much more!

Time spent honestly looking over what things you spend money on today could mean a better life for you and your family tomorrow.

Start including in your calculations how it will feel to be able to pay for a child's education without worry, to take the family on a vacation without worry, and to have the freedom of time to travel the world with your partner rather than travel around your own city.

That said, I am actually not suggesting that you need to stop spending on all of the wants and luxuries that you enjoy. What I am saying is that being financially fit means being able to indulge any of the desires and luxuries that you can fit within your budget. But you must not live above your means.

In other words *pay yourself first* and then spend what's left.

The key is to live within your means: only go on holidays that are within your means, only buy a car that is within your budget.

If there are more wants that you feel are important to you, then you need to figure out how you can earn more, or free up more cash, to give you the ability to have them, but only after you have *paid yourself first.*

Remember that you are in control – but…you cannot have everything.

Living within your means is about you deciding what is truly important to you and prioritising where you spend your money.

A.B.C.D.E.F of Money Management

The key to living within your means is to set limits on your spending.

This can either be done in a hard way, or an easy way.

The easy way is to separate your expenses into broad categories, and then create a structure around them that is running automatically.

Let me explain by reintroducing the A.B.C.D.E.F. of Money Management from Book Two.

Money management can be summarized and understood by the letters A.B.C.D.E.F.

Consider the following formula:

$$E - A = B + C + D + F$$

Let me expand:

Earned income minus *Abundant or surplus cash* = *Basic expenses* plus *Children's expenses* plus *Debt costs* plus *Flexible expenses*

Earned income is the money that you earn from your work or personal exertion.

Abundant or *surplus cash* is the money that you can put aside for your future needs (the money you use to *pay yourself first*).

Basic expenses are what it costs for your basic needs, such as basic [not luxury] food, shelter and clothing. This does not include spending sprees on new shoes, brand names, or sales. That type of spending should be included in flexible expenses. I also do not count the costs of housing loans in this category, as this is a debt cost, and one that I want you to eliminate as soon as you reasonably can.

Children's expenses are the costs or expenses that you have when raising your children. I like to consider it as a separate category for a couple of reasons. Firstly, your basic expenses increase when your children are financially dependent on you, as do your flexible expenses. Secondly, you have a new expense category in education costs. Most importantly though, by keeping this as a separate category it allows you track the decrease to your cost of living when your children are out of school and no longer a financial drain on your income.

Debt costs are the monthly costs that pay for your loans. It is vitally important that you separate these expenses out, so that you can see exactly how much of your take-home pay is being absorbed by these costs. This is often where you can find big chunks of cash being wasted every month in interest costs for consumer debts and large home mortgages!

Flexible expenses are what you spend on the 'wants' of your life. These are not basic needs – even if you argue that you cannot live without them, the reality is that they are still flexible. If you really had to, you could cut out or reduce some, or all of these expenses, and life would still go on.

The *second step* in the money management system is to list where you are currently spending your money, and then to allocate these expenses into the categories above (i.e. are they a basic expense, children's expense, debt cost, fixed expense, etc.).

The *third step* is to look closely at each expense and identify areas that you could reduce or cut-out all together.

It is very common when people start applying the *Financially Fit Money Management System* that they begin to see better ways of allocating the money they already have, not to mention come up with new ways to earn more income.

They will often find cash by looking at how much money they are giving to the banks through mortgage payments, other loan payments, and credit card interest every month. By aggressively reducing debt, which will be covered later, you can often free up *thousands* of dollars that can then be applied to achieving financial freedom and improving your peace of mind.

While it may take a few years to actually terminate your mortgage; a refinance and a debt termination plan involving your other debts can free up a large amount of cash-flow in a matter of just weeks or months.

The *fourth step* is then to total up the potential savings you have identified in step three, and see if it enough for you to reach your *Pay Yourself First* amount.

Most people are pleasantly surprised to see that there is often more than enough identified savings to be able to confidently set-up a regular *automatic* Pay Yourself First amount.

If after an honest, hard look you can see that you cannot reach your savings goal, then see where you can start – and start there.

The *final step* is to set-up a task or action items list on what you need to cancel or cut-out, and what your weekly spending limit is on the various items.

Remember my view is that budgets don't work. What does work is to *pay yourself first*.

The main aim of the money management system is to help you see that you do have the ability to pay yourself first.

Most people are surprised to discover that they definitely could be paying themselves first, but are surprised to see how much money just seems to evaporate out of their wallets on a myriad of small expenses such as pricy lunches, gourmet coffees, and so on.

Just setting some weekly limits in these areas can bring back as much as a few hundred dollars each and every month. By prioritizing what you spend your money on, most people do not even notice the difference in their lifestyle within 90 days. In fact you may even have more fun taking more care and pride on choosing what deserves your hard earned cash.

Chapter 5
What you need to do

Step 1 – Pay Yourself First – Work out your PYF amount

The first thing you need to do is to set a specific amount that you need to *Pay Yourself First*.

For this step use a minimum of 20% of your before tax income as we discussed in Book Two. (As a Financially Fit client, we will assist you to calculate your specific PYF amount based on where you are now, and your personal Financial Freedom goals.)

Let me start with an example:

John and Mary are both 35 years old, both are employed, and they earn a combined income before tax of $10,000 per month.

1. How much do John & Mary earn each month before tax? $10,000 per month.

2. Calculate John & Mary's *Pay Yourself First* amount:

Multiply your monthly before tax earnings (from above) by 20%
Earning $10,000 x 20% = $2,000 PYF monthly amount

3. Does your employer make any contributions to your retirement account? Yes
John and Mary live in Australia where their employer makes a mandatory contribution of 9.25% of their before tax earnings into their Superannuation (retirement) account.

If Yes, how much does your employer contribute each month? $925 per month

4. Calculate the PYF amount that John & Mary need to achieve.
PYF amount (from above) minus Employer Contributions equals PYF amount that John & Mary are responsible for.

Total PYF amount $2,000 - Employer PYF $925 = **John & Mary's PYF amount is $1,075 each month.**

Okay, now it is your turn.

1. How much do you earn each month before tax?_____

2. Calculate your *Pay Yourself First* amount:

Multiply your monthly before tax earnings (from above) by 20%
Earning _____ x 20% = _____PYF amount

3. Does your employer make any contributions to your retirement account? Yes / No

If Yes, how much does your employer contribute each month?_____

4. Calculate the PYF amount that you need to achieve.

PYF amount (from above) minus Employer Contributions equals PYF amount that you are responsible for.

Total PYF amount_____ - Employer PYF _____ = **Your PYF amount** _____**each month.**

Congratulations!

You now have a specific amount to be *Paying Yourself First*.

Make sure that you write this down, as this is the vital lifeblood that you will need to activate the rest of the plan.

Important note – Don't panic if you don't know if you can actually commit to paying that amount at this stage. Once we have worked through the next few steps together, you can always come back and start at a lower number, and aim to gradually increase it as your Financial Health improves.

Step 2 – Living within your means

There are 3 steps to predictable be able to live within your means.

They are:

1. Work out where you are spending your money right now.
2. Step priorities and limits on where you will spend your money.
3. Setting up the right banking structures and cash-flows to allow you to easily identify when you are potentially going to break those limits.

Where does your money go right now?

Now that you have your *Pay Yourself First* number the next step is to get an idea of where your money goes right now.

What I would like you to do is write down how much you spend per month on each of the areas below (where the expense is not a monthly expense, work out how much it costs you each year, and then divide that number by 12 to get your monthly expense number).

Make this as accurate as possible, but don't worry too much if you don't know the exact number – a reasonable estimate will be good enough for this step.

(You can find a budget spreadsheet that you can use for this exercise at www.wealthtoday.com.au under Free Resources.)

What you Spend

Debts	Amount
Home Mortgage	
Investment Debts	
Credit Card	
Personal Loan	
Other Debts	

Housing

Rent	
Council rates	
Body Corporate fees	
Building/Contents Insurance	
Maintenance	
Electricity	
Gas	
Water	
Pay TV	
Other	

Communication

Internet	
Home phone	
Mobile phone(s)	

Transport

Car insurance	
Car maintenance	
Car rego / Licence	
Petrol	
Parking/Tolls etc.	

Trains / Buses / Ferries

Shopping

Groceries/Food

Personal care

Clothing / Shoes

Newspaper / Magazines

Gifts and others

Pets

Education

School/Uni fees

Other Education Expenses

Childcare / Pre-school

Health

Gym / Sporting Membership

Health & Personal Insurances

Doctors/Dentist/Vet

Medicines/Eye care/Other

Travel & Entertainment

Holidays	
Meals Out	
Movies / Music	
Alcohol	
Cigarettes	
Activities	
Other	

Other Expenses

Donations / Charity	
Adviser Fees	
Child support payments	
Other	

Now add all the amounts up to get your **Total Expenses** $_____

Step 3 – Where can you find savings?

The next step is to identify areas where you can spend less.

Remember that you are in control of this process. This is about you determining where your priorities lie – are you serious about wanting to become financially fit? If so, a little bit of discipline now will give you a lot more freedom later.

Go through each item in the budget worksheet & look for areas where you can save, cut back, or cut out completely.

	New Amount (after saving/cut back)
Debts	
Home Mortgage	
Investment Debts	
Credit Card	
Personal Loan	
Other Debts	

Housing	
Rent	
Council rates	
Body Corporate fees	
Building/Contents Insurance	
Maintenance	
Electricity	
Gas	

Water

Pay TV

Other

Communication

Internet

Home phone

Mobile phone(s)

Transport

Car insurance

Car maintenance

Car rego / Licence

Petrol

Parking/Tolls etc.

Trains / Buses / Ferries

Shopping

Groceries/Food

Personal care

Clothing / Shoes

Newspaper / Magazines

Gifts and others

Pets

Education

School/Uni fees

Other Education Expenses

Childcare / Pre-school

Health

Gym / Sporting Membership

Health & Personal Insurances

Doctors/Dentist/Vet

Medicines/Eye care/Other

Travel & Entertainment

Holidays

Meals Out

Movies / Music

Alcohol

Cigarettes

Activities

Other

Other Expenses

Donations / Charity	
Adviser Fees	
Child support payments	
Other	

Now add all the amounts up to get your **New Total Expenses** $_____

What were your **Original Total Expenses?** $_____ (This is the amount before you looked for savings).

Now subtract Original Total Expenses from New Total Expenses: _____

This is the amount of your potential savings.

Step 4 – Is it enough to reach your PYF amount?

Are you surprised by how much is potentially available to save?

When most people truly do the previous exercise properly, they are surprised by how much money they are wasting each month.

When you try to save after you have paid everyone else first, it is amazing how many little, and not so little, 'wants' can disguise themselves as things that we 'need'.

This is why it is absolutely imperative that you make the commitment to *'Pay Yourself First'*. This is the way to be sure that you are putting financial security and freedom at the top of your priorities.

Write down your potential savings from Step 3 previously:_____.

Now also write down your *Pay Yourself First* goal amount from Step 1 _____.

Have you found enough savings and areas where you can cut back expenses to reach your *Pay Yourself First* goal amount?

If the answer is no, then go back and have a closer look for more savings in the budget worksheet. Come on…I know there are a few more 'wants' hiding in there that you can shake out.

Big tip– have a look at how much you are currently giving the banks in loan payments.

Total up the amount of money you are paying on debts each month and write it here: _____

Now add that to your potential savings from Step 3: _____

Is that total number higher than your *'Pay Yourself First'* goal amount? There is a very good chance that the answer to this question is *"Hell yes!"*.

What does this mean?

It means that the thing that is really holding you back and is the cause of most people's financial stress is the amount of debt they have!

Your debt is sucking up so much of your money each month that unless we kill it, it will almost certainly kill you financially!

This is why it is vital to find the areas that you can make savings now, so that you can *'Pay Yourself First'*.

A large portion of the PYF amount will be going towards terminating your debts with extreme prejudice!

Step 5 – Restructure your Bank Accounts

In this step we are going to put in place cash-flow channels and structures to make it a lot easier to know when you are overspending, and equally to have the peace-of-mind when you are spending money that you are *Living within your Means*.

We do this by having different bank accounts for each of the major spending types that you have.

This is the electronic equivalent to separating your money out into different jars for different bills and expenses (do you remember your parents or your grandparents doing that?)

Let's start by identifying the different accounts you have at the moment.

List your current bank accounts and credit cards

_____
_____
_____
_____
_____
_____
_____
_____
_____
_____

What are each of those accounts for?

Write down the purpose of each account next to where they are listed above.

Now let's look at whether you have the right account structure to make it easier to be Financially Fit.

Do you have a Pay Yourself First account?

This is the account that one of my friends calls "When the sh*t hits the fan account" – in other words it is for when you have a real disaster (note, by this I mean something like a medical emergency, or losing your job). If not, then I recommend that you set one up. The aim will be to get this account to an absolute minimum of 3 months worth of living expenses as fast as possible, if you are not already there.

Are you self-employed?

If yes, do you already have a separate account to hold the tax money that you need to pay to the government (for example PAYG and GST monies in Australia)? If not, then I recommend you set-up a "Tax Account" to keep this money separate from your other monies.

Do you ever get caught out by irregular bills (expenses that don't come in monthly, for example school expenses, car servicing and registration, water and electricity, etc.)?

If yes, I recommend that you set-up a separate Irregular Expense Account (call it IREA Account). I'll be going through how much you should be putting into this account in the next section.

Do you have any holiday, car or other big-ticket purchases or expenses planned?

If yes, I recommend that you set-up a separate account (call it Future Goals Account) to save for these expenses. They have a nasty habit of creeping up on you and blowing a hole in your budget and savings. If you have several major future expenses coming up over the next two to three years, for example a wedding, overseas holiday, and a plan to replace your car, then it can be a good idea to set up a separate account for each event so that you can more easily track your progress.

Which account does your salary currently go into?
Is this the same account that you spend from everyday?

If yes, then I recommend that you setup a different everyday account. This should allow you to build up a small buffer in your salary account to cover some minor unexpected bills such as minor car repairs, dental etc.

Do you use a credit card (or more than one) for everyday expenses?
Do you pay them off in full every month?

If not then I recommend that you stop using it immediately and consider it a debt that needs to be paid off in full and closed.

If you cannot pay your credit card off every month and still *Pay Yourself First*, then I recommend that you attach a debit card (one with no credit or borrowing limit) to your everyday account. By doing this you can still use Visa or MasterCard facilities when you need them, but you are only spending money you have, rather than borrowed money.

Have a look at the diagram below for a visual example of an ideal account layout. The arrows in the diagram also show how your money will flow through the accounts.

Ideal Account Structure

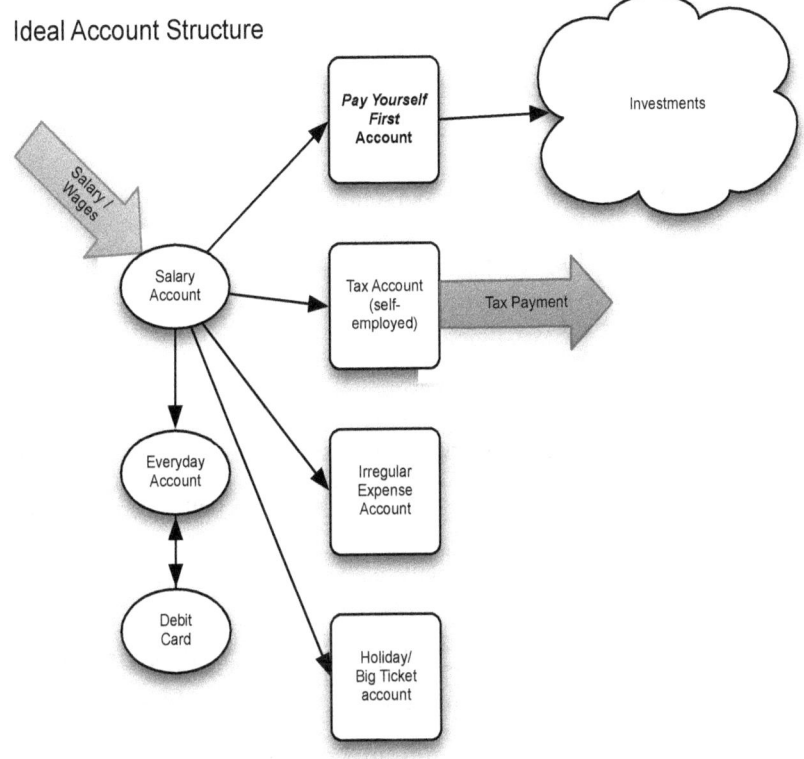

Step 6 – Calculating the amounts to go into each account

Now that you have the right account structures set-up, the next step in becoming Financially Fit is to calculate the amounts that need to be going into each account.

Salary Account – This is simple. All of your earned income (the money you have to go to work for) should be deposited into this account.

Think of this account as your personal financial controller account. It should have all the money coming into it (except for the money your investments make – that will be dealt with separately).

Also importantly this account should have no direct debits or other expenses coming out of it, other than the regular payments for your loans (except credit cards that you are still using) and the deposits that will go into the other accounts.

Pay Yourself First (PYF) Account – In Step 1 of this chapter you worked out your PYF amount. This is the amount that should be set up to be automatically deposited from your Salary Account into your PYF Account 72 hours after your pay is normally due to arrive in your Salary Account.

Your PYF amount _____ each month.

Tax Account – If you are self-employed, this account is to keep the tax money that you need to pay the government separate from your other money.

How much should go into this account?

A simple way is to look at how much tax you had to pay last year.

If nothing has changed this year then simply divide the amount by 12 if paying monthly to get the regular amount to contribute to this account (Option 1).

If you have a large seasonal variation in your income, then you can work out a percentage and transfer that amount at each income period. This is not my preferred option however, as it requires you to manually calculate and transfer your tax amount each time (Option 2).

Option 1 (preferred) – If you paid $24,000 in tax last year for example, then the amount to transfer each month is $24,000 divided by 12 = $2,000 per month.

Your Tax amount _____ each month (Option 1).

Option 2 – If you earned say $100,000 last year, and paid $24,000 in tax, then your average tax paid was $24,000 divided by $100,000 = 24%.

To calculate the amount to transfer each month multiply average tax paid (e.g. 24%) by the amount of money you received within that month. For example if in one month you received $10,000, then the amount to transfer is $10,000 x 24% = $2,400. If in another month you received $5,000, then the amount to transfer is $5,000 x 24% = $1,200.

Your Tax percentage _____% each month (Option 2).

<u>Irregular Expense Account</u> – This account is to have money set aside to pay for expenses that are not monthly, for example school fees or car registration.

If you don't have money set aside for these there is a good chance that they will trip you up when they are due to be paid.

To work out how much you should set aside let's go back to your budgeted amounts that you worked out in Step 3. In the list below, write down whether each expense is a regular (monthly or more frequent), or irregular expense (occurs less often than monthly).

Debts	Amount	Regular / Irregular
Home Mortgage		
Investment Debts		
Credit Card		
Personal Loan		
Other Debts		

Housing

Rent		
Council rates		
Body Corporate fees		
Building/Contents Insurance		
Maintenance		
Electricity		
Gas		
Water		
Pay TV		
Other		

Communication

Internet		
Home phone		
Mobile phone(s)		

Transport

Car insurance		
Car maintenance		
Car rego / Licence		
Petrol		

Parking/Tolls etc.		
Trains / Buses / Ferries		

Shopping

Groceries/Food		
Personal care		
Clothing / Shoes		
Newspaper / Magazines		
Gifts and others		
Pets		

Education

School/Uni fees		
Other Education Expenses		
Childcare / Pre-school		

Health

Gym / Sporting Membership		
Health & Personal Insurances		
Doctors/Dentist/Vet		
Medicines/Eye care/Other		

Travel & Entertainment

Holidays	
Meals Out	
Movies / Music	
Alcohol	
Cigarettes	
Activities	
Other	

Other Expenses

Donations / Charity	
Adviser Fees	
Child support payments	
Other	

Add all the *Irregular* amounts up to get your Monthly Irregular Expense Amount $_____

This is the amount that you need to transfer each month to be able to have enough money set aside to pay for your irregular expenses as and when they are due to be paid.

At this time, also add up the *Regular* amounts up to get your Monthly Regular Expense Amount $_____

This amount will be used in the next section.

Everyday Account – This account is what you use to pay for your regular monthly or more frequent payments, and your incidental and luxury expenses. In the section above we calculated the amount to be transferred into this account each month.

Monthly Regular Expense Amount $_____.

Future Goals Account – Not planning and properly catering for large future expenses is one of the main reasons that people go into debt.

For example if your car needs to be replaced, and you haven't put an appropriate amount of money aside, it is most likely that you will fall for borrowing money to pay for the car. This can end up seriously derailing or slowing down your Financial Fitness plan.

So let's now look at what future goals or expenses you have on the horizon.

Write down the goal, the amount of money you will need, and when you will need it by.

Then in the 4th column break the goal down into a monthly savings goal as I've shown in the example below:

Goal / Planned Expense	Amount	When? (in months)	Monthly Amount (Amount divided by number of months)
e.g. Replace car	$10,000	3 years (36 months)	$10,000 / 36 = $278/mth

Now total up the monthly amounts to get the amount you need to set aside into your Future Goals account:

Monthly amount $_____.

*Note may find it easier to have several Future Goals accounts to keep track of your progress towards important future goals separately (e.g. Holiday, new car, wedding, house saving, kids school or college fund).

Step 7 – Managing your money-flow automatically

Okay, at this point if you have taken the time to do the above exercises you should have the following:

- Your bank account structures set-up
- Know the amount to transfer to each account

The key to having financial piece of mind is to set this up to run automatically.

Ideally you do not want to be trying to remember what amounts you are supposed to be transferring into each of the accounts every payday.

So now we need to switch the engines on so that the plan will run without you having to think about it.

Follow these 8 steps to put this into place:

1. Make sure that your income is set to go into your Salary Account.

2. Set up a direct debit for your Pay Yourself First amount to come out of your Salary Account and flow into your PYF Account automatically 3 days after your salary arrives (to allow for any delays to be weekends or holidays).

3. Set up a direct debit for your Tax amount to come out of your Salary Account and flow into your Tax Account automatically 3 days after your salary arrives.

4. Set up a direct debit for your Irregular Expense amount to come out of your Salary Account and flow into your Irregular Expense Account automatically 3 days after your salary arrives.

5. Set up a direct debit for your Everyday amount to come out of your Salary Account and flow into your Everyday Account automatically 3 days after your salary arrives.

6. Set up a direct debit for your Future Goals amount to come out of your Salary Account and flow into your Future Goals Account automatically on 3 days after your salary arrives.

7. Set up for any regular debt or loan payments to come out of your Salary Account.

8. Make sure that any direct debits for other expenses only come out of your Everyday Account.

Step 8 – Close unnecessary accounts

Now make sure that you close any unnecessary accounts. In particular any credit cards that you do not clear every month within your Everyday expense amount.

Step 9 – Commit to your Financial Health

The above plan works if you commit to setting it up properly, and following it.

The two commitments that you need are:

1. To stop spending when you run out of money in your Everyday Account.

Do not fall into the trap of stealing from another account when in reality you are just spending too much.
Make the commitment to live within your means.
You can spend the money in your Everyday Account however you like, on whatever you like, as long as you do not spend any more than the amount you have allocated as your Everyday Expense amount.

2. Do not go into any more debt.

Make the commitment that under no circumstances will you go into any more debt; no matter how good 'the deal' looks.

This includes no more spending on credit cards unless you can clear them each and every month within your Everyday expense allocation. Also definitely no 'interest free' purchases, no 'buy now, pay later' deals....you get the idea.

If you can commit to these two things you will find that within 90 days you have become used to living within your means on the new amounts, and it seem completely normal.

You will also very quickly find that irregular expenses no longer trip you up, and that you are becoming financially stronger every day.

What do you do if there isn't enough money to go around?

What do you do if you find out that your budget doesn't balance? You have gone through the above numbers, and there just isn't enough to go around. What do you do?

This can happen.

For many people they run their lives on a day-to-day, week-to-week, month-to-month basis. Where they get unstuck is in irregular expenses and future goals that they haven't provided for.

So what usually happens is they go into debt (either by paying on their credit cards, or getting a loan) to pay for these unplanned for expenses.

These debts then need to be paid back including interest each month, meaning that now they have even less surplus cash-flow each month.

When the next round of irregular expenses or future goals become due, they now have even less ability to pay for them, meaning they get even deeper into debt and making it harder to dig themselves out of it.

It usually starts with people confusing needs versus wants, and spending beyond their means.

Unless this is brought into check, eventually they will have no spare money available and will find that their way of life is under threat.

So what do you do if you find there is not enough money to cover your needs and wants, paying yourself first and your future goals?

Well to be absolutely frank, you have some tough decisions to make.

Something has to give!

You will need to:

- increase your income enough to cover all the above;
- cut back further on your needs and wants;
- reduce, delay or cut-out some of your future goals;
- reduce the income you expect to live on in retirement, or delay the age at which you wish to be financially free; or
- commit to a combination of all of the above.

There are obviously some sacrifices to be made.

The reality is that you are where you are because of the choices you have made, or you have allowed others to make for you in the past.

You can get back on track and become financially fit quite quickly, but in some cases it may take tightening the belt a little more than is comfortable, at least in the early stages whilst you are killing your debt.

Imagine.....

If it feels a little tough in the beginning, have a look at how you will be able to accelerate once we are into the swing.

Consider what your PYF number will be when:

1. You have no more debt.

Imagine when you are no longer paying money to the banks each month. Imagine what you can do with that extra money.

2. If you currently have children that are dependent on you – eventually (hopefully) they will grow up, and be paying their own way.

How much will your expenses reduce when this happens?

Imagine what you can also do with that extra money.

I bring these points up for a reason. It is not where you start that matters so much as the destination that you are going to.

If you work the plan that I am showing you, you will whip your finances into shape in no time at all.

With each step you take you will be strengthening your Financial Health, and accelerating down the path to Financial Freedom.

Do your best.

Start wherever you are today.

Do the best with what you have currently got, but start NOW!!!

Over the coming days, weeks and months look for ways that you can make small (and larger) increases to the amount you can set aside to *Pay Yourself First*.

This will steadily start to compound (remember the earlier demonstration of the power of Compound Interest?), and step-by-step start to accelerate and snowball.

Chapter 6
Graduating Stage One

You can actually measure your journey to Financial Freedom.

If you correctly action each of the steps suggested in this book, not only will you become Financially Fit, but also you will progressively move towards Financial Independence and Freedom.

A good friend of mine, Iain Tait, has a quote that I've used in business for years – he says:

"What you measure you can manage."

What he means is that it is important to regularly monitor your progress. It is also important to set up milestones, or intermediate goals that need to be achieved on the way to your major goal.

The major goal is to achieve *Financial Freedom* – to have your investment assets making you enough income to pay for your monthly expenses.

The first milestone or intermediate goal to celebrate is the achievement of becoming *Financially Fit*. This is the first major step towards Financial Freedom, and is the stepping-stone to all the other stages.

So how do you graduate from Stage One (and be able to say that you are Financially Fit)?

How do you know when you are Financially Fit?

Stage One is about the practical application of the first two Principles of Wealth:

To Pay Yourself First; and
To Live Within Your Means.

You graduate to being *Financially Fit* by having these principles correctly working for you in your life.

You measure it by achievement of the following outcomes:

1. Paying Yourself First - You are paying no less than 20% of your before tax income into your PYF account every month *automatically*.

2. Living within your means:

a. You have set up your Bank Account correctly

b. You have calculated and set up the amounts to transfer to each of the accounts *automatically*.

c. You have closed any unnecessary accounts.

d. You are paying off your credit card/s each month from your Everyday account; or if not you have stopped using (and cut up) your credit cards.

If you have accomplished the above goals, then congratulations, you are now *Financially Fit!*

Stage Two

Moving up to being *Financially Secure*

Chapter 7

What you need to know

What is the goal of Stage Two – becoming *Financially Secure?*

Financial Security is about the practical application of Rule 4 – Protecting Yourself.

The focus of *Stage Two* is to build a secure safety net under you and your family that is able to withstand the majority of financial shocks that life may unexpectedly deliver.

Before you can seriously consider and act against plans to become *Financially Independent* or *Financially Free* it is very important to de-risk your life.

What I mean by that is to recognise that unexpected things can happen at any point, and sometimes bad things can happen to good people.

The goal of Stage Two is to build safety nets that are able to withstand these shocks to a large extent.

This does several things.

Firstly it can give you amazing peace of mind, reduce worry about what might happen, and stay focused on the more important things in your lives.

The second thing is that you can have the comfort of knowing that if something drastic does happen, that this may very well <u>accelerate</u> your journey to Financial Independence (and at least leave your partner or family financially independent).

As soon as you have identified your *Pay Yourself First* amount from Stage One, you should work through this Stage to ensure that you are adequately protected as soon as possible.

These safety nets are the first priority for the surplus cash you create from Stage One.

There are 3 key components in being *Financially Secure*:

1. Having an Emergency Cash Buffer

2. Having the right type and amounts of personal insurances in place to cover any gaps in your safety net

3. Having a Debt Termination Strategy underway

This stage should be able to be well underway within 90 to 120 days of starting your Financial Fitness plan.

Let's consider them in the order above.

1. Emergency Cash Buffer - The first step in building Wealth

You will recall from Stage One that I also called the *Pay Yourself First Account* the *Emergency Buffer account.*

Many people I come across are far more financially vulnerable than they realize. In many cases if their income suddenly stopped, they would run out of money in less than 4 weeks.

If your income stopped how long could you still pay the bills and eat?

If the answer is less than 90 days (3 months) you are very vulnerable and this needs serious attention.

If the answer is more than 90 days then congratulations.

What do I mean by an Emergency Buffer?

I mean that you have a cash lump sum that is equal to at least 3 months of living expenses set aside in a <u>separate account</u>.

For this purpose your Living Expenses includes your fixed debt repayments, and basic living expenses, as well as any expenses that you cannot immediately cut-out if you had to.

The account that contains this cash lump sum should allow you to access the money within 24-48 hours, but should specifically <u>not</u> have a checkbook, bankcard or credit card linked to it.

You should not be able to access the money in any way other than a carefully considered online withdrawal into another account, a fax or in-bank branch withdrawal application.

In other words, it should be relatively hard to get access to the money. Its purpose is solely to give you a small safety buffer in the event of a sudden disruption to your income or true emergency that you couldn't have predicted or allowed for.

2. Personal Insurances

Ultimately the best protection will come from having strong portfolio of working investments that build an impenetrable financial wall around you and your family.

Until that time, however, it is important to have the right mix of personal insurances in place as part of your effective safety net.

Most of us know of or can think of people close to us who have had unexpected things happen to them, such as an accident, cancer, stroke or heart attack.

Most of them did not expect anything bad to happen to them either, but it often happens without warning and is usually very traumatic to them (assuming they survive at least for a while) and their family. In particular it can have devastating financial consequences if the right safety nets aren't in place.

My sincere hope is that the money you spend on insurance turns out to be a complete waste, because this will mean that you have enjoyed a long and healthy life.

However, we cannot be sure of that, so for this reason alone it is important to make sure that you and your family are covered against unexpected events.

"How much insurance cover do I really need?"

The answer to the question is just enough but not too much.

Calculating the right amount of cover for you involves considering a number of factors.

An essential element in determining your insurance needs is to consider how much financial risk you personally want to carry, and how much would you like to give to another company for a (relatively) small monthly fee.

In the next chapter you will be doing some fairly simple calculations. The aim of this is to see the size of any potential gaps in your safety net.

You can then decide how much of that risk you want to personally take, and how much you would prefer to give to another (insurance) company.

Part of this for you to clarify what you would like to happen if an unexpected event occurred. Obviously the other important consideration is how much it would cost to purchase the insurances that would cover the gaps in your safety net.

Many people don't fully understand that this is the true purpose of insurances.

Unscrupulous salesmen have oversold much insurance over the years, and as a result people are suspicious of this area. This has left people not realising the extent to which they are personally underinsured (something they would never let happen to their car), and incredibly exposed to events that are actually quite common.

What I aim to do in this section is to demystify the area of insurances.

By the end of this section you should be able to quite methodically and scientifically calculate the amount of type of the various insurances that you may need.

This will then allow you to be actively involved in knowing how much cover you want, and how much you will need to pay for the right amount of cover.

This is a very empowered way to know exactly what your insurance is designed to cover.

If you are currently is good health, this can be one of the most compelling reasons to put the insurances you need in place now (while you still have good health). If you aren't in good health you may very well find that you cannot get the insurances you need, or that it is a lot more expensive. Once your insurance policies are in place, your insurer generally cannot cancel it, as long as you keep up with the payments.

As you build wealth you should progressively need *less* insurance as the gap in your safety net gradually reduces as your Financial Health increases.

3. Debt Termination Plan – Killing off that damn debt!

So many people that I see will never be able to become *Financially Free* solely due to how much their monthly debt payments are costing them.

It is not unusual to see people from all walks of life giving more than *half* of their take home pay to the banks in debt repayments every month.

That is crazy!

How can you hope to get ahead if half your money is going to the banks before you can blink!

Are your personal debts strangling your chance of success?

It is absolutely essential that you kill off that damn debt and get your money back so you can send it out to work for you, and not the banks.

The third key part of becoming *Financially Secure* is to have an effective *Debt Termination Plan* in place.

In the next chapter you will be setting up a plan to terminate your debts with extreme prejudice.

Should I get out of debt, or build wealth first?

Great question. The simple answer is that you need to do both.

Being in debt does 2 things:

1. It takes hard earned money out of your pocket every month that you should be using to become Financially Free; and

2. It increases the minimum amount you need to be earning each month just to cover your living expenses..

This pushes the goal of *Financial Freedom* further away.

In other words if you are carrying debt then you need your investments to be earning you your minimum monthly living requirements AND your debt repayments before you are Financially Free.

Okay, so it may seem that focuses on paying off debt first is the way to go.

Not so.

If you just pay off debt here is what happens:

1. You are still very financially vulnerable as there is a very likely probability that your emergency buffer is not at minimum levels.

This means that any bump in the road can derail your plans and send you back to square one.

2. Once you have paid off debt you still don't have any investments that are putting money into your pocket.

This means that you are actually no closer to becoming financially independent or free.

I find that the healthy balance is to do a combination of both.

This is not just healthy financially, but healthy mentally and emotionally as well.

When you are both paying off debt and building wealth each month you see both your debt going down AND your wealth going up…and that starts to feel real good!

The healthy balance that I usually suggest you start with is a ratio of 2/3 and 1/3. Two thirds of your *Pay Yourself First* amount should go to terminating your debts and the remaining one third to building wealth.

In the next chapter you will be working out what is the right balance for you.

Chapter 8

What you need to do

Step 1 - PYF Account - How big should your Emergency Cash Buffer Be?

Before you look at building investments you should have a minimum of 3 months of expenses set aside to cover any real emergencies.

To work this out you will need to look back at the budget you completed in Step 3 of the first Stage – Financially Fit.

What was your *New Total Expenses*?

Write the monthly figure here:_____.

Now have a look through your budget and think about which of the expenses are flexible expenses that you could immediately cut out or cut back if an emergency arose.

Add up those expenses and write the monthly figure here:_____.

Now subtract that figure from your monthly Total Expenses figure above:_____(minimum monthly expense).

This figure is the monthly minimum expenses that you will still need to pay even if your income suddenly stopped.

Now multiply this by three:

Minimum monthly expense_____ X 3 = _____.

This amount is your Emergency Cash Buffer goal.

The first use of your *Pay Yourself First Account* is to serve as the place where you store your Emergency Cash Reserve.

Once this amount has been achieved you can then look to also begin building your investments from this account as well.

I'll be going into that more in Stage Four – Financially Free.

Step 2 – Personal Insurance - How much do you really need?

Did You Know?

The most common reason for retiring or permanently stopping work is poor health - particularly in those that have stopped working at a relatively young age (almost 80% of those who retired before forty-five years of age) (Source: ABS)

The second essential part of becoming *Financially Secure* is ensuring that you and your family are adequately protected if anything goes wrong.

This requires thinking about what you would want and need to have happen in various events (e.g. cannot work due to a medical condition, or one of you die unexpectedly).

Next consider your ability to self-insure – this means how much risk you are able to withstand yourself due to the strength of your current investments and passive income streams.

You will most probably find that there is a gap between what you want to have happen and you ability to realistically cover that yourself.

Over time we aim to show you how to reduce that gap, but until then it is a good idea to get the right mix of personal insurances to cover it.

The key to Financial Security in this step is to get just the right amount of cover for your needs budget…not too much and not too little.

So how do we do that?

The aim of insurance cover is not to try to cover every obscure possibility or treatment option, nor to make insurance like a type of lottery win.

The aim <u>is</u> to put in place an effective and affordable safety net that covers you against likely possibilities and treatment options and is not just affordable now, but in particular is affordable enough to have in place when you are most likely to be needing it (the most likely age to make a claim for trauma cover is 49 years of age *source Asteron Life)

Personal Insurance breaks down into two main groups:

1. Income Protection insurance
2. Insurance that pays you cash lump sums
   Life Insurance
   Disability Insurance
   Trauma Insurance

1. Income Protection
Start by considering protecting your income.

Income protection insurance protects your income earning ability.

In Australia this can usually cover up to seventy-five percent of the income you earn from your personal exertion, if you are unable to work due to medical reasons.

It can also cover a number of business expenses as well. Many countries around the world have equivalent types of insurance available.

This is a particularly vital insurance that is often overlooked. Your ability to earn an income is the key factor in being able to provide for your family today, as well as save for the future.

Ask yourself the following question:

- If your income stopped today, how long could you keep living your current lifestyle?

If your answer is not – "indefinitely", then you seriously need to consider getting income protection in place.

Let's calculate the amount of income protection cover you can get. (Note this is done from a perspective of Australia, however if you are in a different country it is likely that your insurances work in a similar fashion).

What is your Monthly Gross Income? (This is your income from working before tax is taken out) _____

Does your employer make minimum compulsory superannuation (retirement) payments? Yes / No

If yes, how much each month? _____(In Australia this is currently 9.25% of your before tax income if you are employed).

Add your Monthly Gross Income and minimum retirement payments:_____

Now multiply it by 0.75 (to get 75%):_____(max. monthly benefit).

This is the maximum monthly amount that you may qualify to get covered by Income Protection insurance.
*Note for self-employed people – a sub-category of income protection is available to cover up to 100% of eligible business expenses usually for a maximum of 1 year. Your adviser will usually need to help you with this.

<u>Period of cover</u> – this is the length of time that the income protection insurance may pay out if you make a claim.

I recommend that you consider getting cover until at least 65 years of age for when your retirement benefits then become available.

<u>Waiting Period</u> – this is the amount of time you will have to wait if you have a claimable event before the income protection insurance will start to pay.

The longer the waiting period usually the cheaper the insurance cover is, but you want to be sure that you can survive the waiting period.

Question: How long could you continue to pay your bills if your income stopped?

If your answer is not more than 4 weeks, then look at selecting a 1-month waiting period (which is the default recommendation).

As your *PYF* account grows to 3 months of living expenses, you can then look at increasing your waiting period to 90 days. This may entitle you to a discount on your insurance payments of up to 40%.

2. Cash Lump Sum Insurance

Insurances that give you cash lump sum payments generally include three categories:

1. Life Insurance: Pays a cash lump sum if you pass away whilst the insurance is in place.

2. Disability Cover: Pays a cash lump sum if you are permanently disabled and unable to ever return to work.

3. Trauma Cover: Pays a cash lump sum if you suffer a particular illness or trauma (e.g. heart attack, cancer or stroke).

Calculating the right amount of insurance cover is similar for each of the above insurances.

There are 3 main parts to think about:

1. How much lump sum cash would you need? (for example – how much you need to pay off debts and other one-off costs)

2. How much ongoing income would you need? (how much ongoing income will you or your family be needing, and for how many years)

3. How much of the risk can (and do you want) to take? (your current ability to insure or take on the risks yourself)

Calculating the right amount for you is then simply a matter at adding 1 & 2 together and then subtracting 3 from it.

I've included a simple method below to calculate approximately how much of each type of insurance cover you need for each of the lump sum insurances.

Note - If you find any of this section too complex, or wish to work out more detailed calculations, or need any other assistance please don't hesitate to contact my team at www.WealthToday.com.au – they are always very happy to help.

1. Life Insurance:
    Take some time now to fill in each of the sections below.

Think about what you would like to financially if you were to pass away unexpectedly.

I know this can be quite an uncomfortable subject to talk about, but it is important to have plans in place to ensure that you and your family are financially protected if something like that did happen.

	Life Insurance Cover
Reason for cover?	If you passed away, what would you want to happen?
Lump Sum Cash Needs	1. Debts: (Suggest all Debts to be cleared) How much do you need/want to pay off debts? $_____ 2. One-off Lump sums: How much do you need/want for Funeral Costs? $_____ How much do you need/want for Financial & Legal expenses? $_____ How much for any other Lump Sum Needs? $_____ Total: $_____ (A)
Ongoing Income	How much income do I need?

Needed	1. What is your Monthly Emergency Expense Amount (from previous section)? $_____ per month 2. How much would your expenses drop after your loans were paid out? $_____ per month 3. How much would you partner still earn (if to continue working)? $_____ per month Subtract 2 and 3 from 1 above to calculate your ongoing income needed. $_____ per month Multiply by 12 $_____ per year (a) How long do you need / want the cover for? (Recommend to age 90) _____ years (b) Total: (a) times (b) = $_____ (B)
Existing Cover	How much Existing Savings do you have? $_____ What are you retirement account (Superannuation) balances? $_____ What is the value of Assets you would sell? $_____ Total: $_____ (C)

Using the information that you have completed above now calculate the gap you currently have in your Life Cover safety net:

(A) Lump Sum Total: $_____

(B) Ongoing Income Total: $_____

Add (A) and (B) together $_____

Now Subtract (C) Existing Cover Total from above.

Total Amount of Life Insurance Cover you need: $_____

Do you have any Life Insurance at the moment? Yes/No

If yes, how much does it cover? $_____

Subtract the Amount of the amount of Life Cover you have at the moment from the amount of Life Insurance Cover you need.

$_____

This number is the gap that you currently have in your safety net if you were to pass away.

2. Disability Cover

Let's do the same now for disability cover.

	Disability Cover
Reason for cover?	If you were permanently disabled and couldn't work again, what would you want to happen?

Lump Sum Cash Needs	**1. Debts:** (Suggest all Debts to be cleared) How much do you need/want to pay off debts? $_____ **2. One-off Lump sums:** How much do you need/want for Medical Diagnosis and Treatment? $_____ How much do you need/want for Lifestyle Modification (e.g. home modifications)? $_____ How much for any other Lump Sum Needs? $_____ Total: $_____(A)
Ongoing Income Needed	**How much income do I need?** 1. What is your Monthly Emergency Expense Amount (from previous section)? $_____ per month 2. How much is your income protection cover? $_____ per month 3. How much would your expenses drop after your loans were paid out? $_____ per month 4. How much would you partner still earn (if to continue working)? $_____ per month Subtract 2, 3 and 4 from 1 above to calculate your ongoing income needed. $_____ per month

	Multiply by 12 $_____ per year (a) How long do you need / want the cover for? (recommend to age 90) _____ years (b) Total: (a) times (b) = $_____ (B)
Existing Cover	How much Existing Savings do you have? $_____ What is the value of Assets you would sell? $_____ Total: $_____ (C)

Using the information that you have completed above now calculate the gap you currently have in your Disability cover safety net:

(A) Lump Sum Total: $_____

(B) Ongoing Income Total: $_____

Add (A) and (B) together $_____

Now Subtract (C) Existing Cover Total from above.

Total Amount of Disability Insurance Cover you need:
$_____

Do you have any Disability Insurance at the moment? Yes/No

If yes, how much does it cover? $_____

Subtract the Amount of the amount of Disability Cover you have at the moment from the amount of Disability Insurance Cover you need.

$_____

This number is the gap that you currently have in your safety net if you were to be permanently disabled and couldn't work again.

3. Trauma Cover

Let's now do the same for trauma cover.

	Trauma Cover
Reason for cover?	If you suffered a trauma or acute medical event, what would you want to happen?
Lump Sum Cash Needs	1. Debts: (Suggest all Lifestyle Debts to be cleared) How much do you need/want to pay off debts? $_____ 2. One-off Lump sums: How much do you need/want for Medical Diagnosis and Treatment? $_____ How much do you need/want for Lifestyle Modification (e.g. home modifications)? $_____ How much for any other Lump Sum Needs? $_____ Total: $_____(A)
Ongoing	How much income do I need?

Income Needed	1. What is your Monthly Emergency Expense Amount (from previous section)? $_____ per month 2. How much is your income protection cover? $_____ per month 3. How much would your expenses drop after your loans were paid out? $_____ per month 4. How much would you partner still earn (if to continue working)? $_____ per month Subtract 2, 3 and 4 from 1 above to calculate your ongoing income needed. $_____ per month Multiply by 12 $_____ per year (a) How long do you need / want the cover for? (recommend 1 year) _____ years (b) Total: A times B = $_____ (B)
Existing Cover	How much Existing Savings do you have? $_____ What is the value of Assets you would sell? $_____ Total: $_____ (C)

Using the information that you have completed above now calculate the gap you currently have in your Trauma cover safety net:

(A) Lump Sum Total: $_____

(B) Ongoing Income Total: $_____

Add A and B together $_____

Now Subtract (C) Existing Cover Total from above.

Total Amount of Trauma Insurance Cover you need:
$_____

Do you have any Trauma Insurance at the moment? Yes/No

If yes, how much does it cover? $_____

Subtract the Amount of the amount of Trauma Cover you have at the moment from the amount of Trauma Insurance Cover you need.

$_____

This number is the gap that you currently have in your safety net if you were to suffer a trauma or acute medical event.

Insurance Safety Net Summary
Well done!

If have taken the time to think about and work through the insurance safety net questions above you now know the size of any gaps in your safety net.

Are you surprised by the size of the gaps?

Many people I work with are staggered to see that the gap is often well over a million dollars.

Were your numbers the same?

Remember that you will likely earn over $4,000,000 during your lifetime.

If something happened that you couldn't work (or died and weren't able to work), that income earning potential will be lost forever, but you or your family's expenses don't just go away…unless you have them covered with the right insurances for the right purposes.

The next step now is to get the insurances in place to cover those gaps.

This is where your financial adviser steps in. Let them know the size of the gap you wish to cover. They will then source an appropriate insurance product, help submit the applications and get the insurances into place on your behalf.

Again, if you would like my team to give you a hand with any of this, just to get in touch with us at www.WealthToday.com.au .

Step 3 – Debt Termination – Killing off that damn debt!

If you have any debts other than perhaps some tax-deductible investment loans, you would do well to put in place a plan to terminate them.

Your monthly debt repayments are arguably the single most important obstacles that will slow or stop you on your path to becoming Financially Free.

How much you are wasting on debt payments each and every month?

Chances are that this is costing you several times more than you are able to save each month.

Imagine if you have no debt. How much extra money would you have available?

Now imagine if you used that money for your Financial Freedom plan.

How much faster do you think you could reach Financial Freedom?

I'm sure you agree that getting out of debt has to be a very high priority.

So how do you do it?

Like anything it requires a specific, measurable plan to follow, and the focus and commitment to becoming debt-free.

Step 1: No more debt!

The first commitment you must make is to not go into any more debt!

If you seriously want to become debt-free you must stop taking on new debt.

This especially includes using credit cards that you cannot pay off in full each and every month. Cut the cards up and put them away until you have paid them out, then close the accounts.

If you feel you need to have the Visa or MasterCard facility, then approach your bank for a debit card (this is a card with no debt attached – it using the money in your account) that is linked to your Everyday account.

Step 2: List all your debt

The next step is to write down all of your debts.

Make sure you include money that you owe anyone, including family members, store cards, any interest-free purchases that still need to be paid out.

Make a list of all of your debts.

1. _____
2. _____
3. _____
4. _____
5. _____
6. _____
7. _____
8. _____
9. _____
10. _____

Now next to each debt write down the amount you still owe and the monthly repayment amount.

Debt Name	Amount still owed	Monthly Payment amount
Example: Car Loan	*$ 14,000*	*$ 435/month*
1.	$	$
2.	$	$
3.	$	$
4.	$	$
5.	$	$

6.	$	$
7.	$	$
8.	$	$
9.	$	$
10.	$	$
Total	$	$

Make sure that you total up the Monthly Payment Amount (3rd Column).

How much does it come to? $_____ per month.

This is the amount of money that you need to get back into your budget.

This money should be going towards YOUR financial future, not the banks profit!

Step 3: Ranking your debt in the order they will be paid off

So let's get serious about terminating the debt with *extreme prejudice*!

There are a number of ways that this can be done. The most important part of any plan though is the commitment to get out of debt.

I'm going to share with you the plan that is simple to follow and understand.

It involves paying off the debts from the loan with the *lowest Amount Still Owed* to the *highest Amount Still Owed*, and cascading the debt payments from one loan to the next so that with each step you accelerate the speed of paying out the next debt.

While some people may argue that mathematically it is better to pay out the highest interest rate first (which is true), what I find is that the positive feeling that you get by paying off the first one or two smaller debts quickly increases the commitment that you feel to follow through on killing off the remaining debt.

For this reason, this is generally my preferred method.

Terminate your debts in the following order:

1. Start with the lowest outstanding balance debt.

Apply two-thirds of your *Pay Yourself First* amount to this debt over and above the minimum monthly payment that you are already making.

Keep making the minimum payments to the other debts whilst you are doing this.

For example:

If your *PYF* amount is $500, then two-thirds is $330 per month.

If your minimum monthly payment for Debt #1 is $150, then you pay the $150, plus $330, making a total payment of $480 per month to Debt #1 until it is terminated.

2. Once the first debt is terminated, start on the second debt.

This time also add the minimum payment that you were making on the first debt (before you terminated it), in addition to the two-thirds of your savings to Debt #2, until it too is terminated.

For example:

If your minimum monthly payment for Debt 2 is $220, then you pay the $220, plus $150 (the payment you were making to Debt #1 before it was terminated), plus the $330 (two-thirds of your monthly savings), making a total payment of $770 per month to Debt #2 until it is also terminated.

3. Repeat this for any additional debts that you have until they are all terminated.

Usually your home mortgage will be the last debt standing.

If you add the extra loan payments that you now have available (because they are all terminated), as well as the two-thirds of your savings, you will be amazed at how many years earlier you will have paid out your mortgage, as well as the ten to hundreds of thousands of dollars in interest payment that you will not have to pay the bank!

Once all of your debts have been terminated, apply *all the payments and the savings amounts* to your investment savings.

Now rank your debts from lowest Amount Still Owed to highest. This will be the order in which you terminate each debt.

Debt Name	Amount still owed	Monthly Payment amount
Example: Car Loan	$ 14,000	$ 435/month
1.	$	$
2.	$	$
3.	$	$
4.	$	$
5.	$	$
6.	$	$
7.	$	$
8.	$	$
9.	$	$
10.	$	$

Total	$	$

Where should your surplus *PYF* money go?

Okay, let's put section 2 together now into a specific plan.

In Chapter 7 we discussed whether you should get out debt, or build wealth first.

You will remember that it is important to do both.

I also suggested that a healthy ratio is to apply 2/3 of your *Pay Yourself First* amount to terminating your debts, and 1/3 to building wealth.

Let's work out what that means for you.

How much is your *PYF* (Pay Yourself First) Amount that you committed to in Chapter 5?
$_____.

1. <u>Wealth Building Amount</u>
How much should be saved into your PYF Account each month (remember that the key is to set this amount to transfer <u>automatically</u> 3 days after your pay is scheduled to arrive)?

The amount I suggest is one third of your PYF Amount.

Let's calculate it.

PYF Amount times 0.33 will equal the amount to transfer.

PYF Amount $_____ x 0.33 = $_____ wealth building amount.

Now you have the number.

The next step is to arrange for the wealth building amount to be transferred automatically into your PYF Account each month.

2. <u>Debt Termination Amount</u>

How much extra should you pay into the first debt over and above the minimum monthly debt payment each month (remember that the key is to set this amount to transfer <u>automatically</u> 3 days after your pay is scheduled to arrive)?

The amount I suggest is two thirds of your PYF Amount.

Let's calculate it.

PYF Amount times 0.67 will equal the amount to transfer.

PYF Amount $_____ x 0.67 = $_____ Debt Termination amount.

Now you have the number.

The next step is to arrange for the debt termination amount to be paid automatically into the first debt you listed above each month until this debt is terminated.

As soon as the first debt is terminated, add and the minimum monthly payment from debt 1 to this debt termination amount and immediately start terminating debt 2.

Keep following this process until all your debts are terminated.

Once all the debts are cleared, take a breath and give yourself a huge pat on the back.

Then add all the debt payments (okay, okay...maybe take small amount out to pamper yourself) and your original debt termination amount to the amount you are paying into your PYF Account each month, and watch how fast you now start accelerating towards Financial Independence and Freedom!

Chapter 9

Graduating to the next stage

So how do you graduate from Stage Two

(and be able to say that you are Financially Secure)?

How do you know when you are Financially Secure?

Stage Two is about the practical application of the fourth Principle of Wealth: To Protect Yourself.

You graduate to Financial Security by having this principle correctly working for you in your life.

You measure it by achievement of the following outcomes in addition to the accomplishments of Stage One- Financially Fit:

1. You have an effective safety net in place:

a. Your PYF Account balance is above your Emergency Cash Buffer goal of 3 months of minimum monthly expenses.

b. You are applying 1/3 of your PFY amount into your PYF Account *automatically* to go towards wealth building.

c. You have calculated and put in place the right mix of personal insurances to cover the gap in your safety net.

2. Debt Termination Plan

a. You have ranked your debt and are applying 2/3 or your PFY amount into the first debt in addition to the minimum monthly payment *automatically*.

b. You have stopped using any credit cards that you do not pay off every month.

c. You have made the firm commitment not to go into any more debt (unless that debt is part of an investment in Stage Four that puts more money into your pocket in positive cash flow than the debt repayments cost each month).

When you have accomplished the above goals, big congratulations you are now *Financially Secure.*

Stage Three

Path to *Financially Independence*

Chapter 10

What you need to know

Congratulations!

Achieving *Financial Fitness* and *Financial Security* are actually the hardest part of becoming *Financially Free*.

The next two stages are actually simpler.

Yes there is complexity in selecting and monitoring the investments, but the principles and philosophies are simpler.

You also have access to more help at this stage.

With clear instructions, your financial coach (if they are appropriately qualified) can do a lot of the research and investment selection for you, and can help you regularly check that they are performing the right functions within your Financial Security and Freedom plan.

So what is Financial Independence about?

The focus of this Stage is around setting up to make sure you are on track to be financially secure by retirement age (assume 65years old).

Remember earlier in the book I defined Financial Independence as 'when you have enough invested assets to be able to last you until at least age 90'.

So how do we focus on this as well as becoming Financially Free? The aim is to go for *Financial Freedom*, and to achieve this <u>before</u> what is considered to be the usual retirement age.

But what if you fall short?

This is where Stage Three – Financial Independence comes in.

This is the safety net that you put place to be sure that at minimum you having enough savings/investments in place last you for 25 years (from age 65 to age 90).

You need to allow for at least 25 years in retirement (to age 90). Why?

Well simply put it is to make it more likely that you will die before you run out of money.

The average lifespan in first world countries is now to live to between 80-85 years of age.

So what if you live longer than that? Good question.

If you only rely on this stage, you will run out on money and have to hope that the government or family and friends are there to support you.

Risky? Absolutely – which is why we need to have this focus in place, but true freedom and choice comes from the next stage – Stage Four.

So how do I put this in place?

The best way for most people to achieve Financial Independence is by using their retirement investment accounts.

The government is very keen to have more of the population be financially independent in their retirement years, and in most countries have set-up various types of special 'Retirement' accounts. In Australia they are called Superannuation funds and in the USA the main type are called 401k's.

This next point is important and will help you understand some of the complex and strange rules that exist around these types of accounts.

The reason the governments have set these up is solely so that *they* do not have to support you in your retirement years. They are not set up to make you well off. They want you to contribute enough so that you are not a burden, but not too much or else they will miss out on tax revenue. So you will frequently see extra incentives to help you boost this account by small to moderate amounts from time to time.

Advantages

Generally you will find that contributions you make up to a certain level can either be made with 'before-tax' money, or is tax deductible.

This benefit alone can give you some of the best investment returns you will ever see, as almost any other investment you make is with money that you have after the tax has already been paid.

In addition you will often find that there are special tax incentives or that some employers will match money that you contribute with additional money.

Take advantage of these wherever possible. Also look for special incentives to make extra contributions on behalf of your partner or spouse.

A good financial adviser and accountant are best placed to help you become aware and benefit from these.

Disadvantages

The main disadvantage of saving or investing using your retirement saving vehicle is that your money is usually locked away until you are reach retirement age.

The second challenge is that governments make frequent changes to the rules around what you can and cannot do with these accounts.

It is most likely that they will increase the age that you can access it, and limit your ability to make lump sum withdrawals. The whole reasoning it to try to make it last longer and reduce the likelihood that you will need to access government social security payments in your retirement years.

This is not completely a bad thing unless you are totally invested in this strategy - in which case you have handed over control of your freedom to the government.

This means that if you want to retire at a younger age or become financially free before retirement age you need to use other methods. I will be going into this in Stage Four.

A Balanced Strategy with Stage Four – Financial Freedom.

The great news is that if you are serious about going for Financial Freedom, you don't need all of you retirement income to come from this section, and in fact I recommend that you do not have all your savings and investments in retirement savings accounts.

For example if you need $50,000 per year to live on in retirement.

To last 25 years you need a retirement nest egg of 25 X $50,000 = $1,250,000 in today's money.

But what if you already have $25,000 in ongoing come in from your investments?

In this case your Financial Independence nest egg just needs to make up the difference - 25 X $25,000 = $625,000

This is much more realistic and achievable over your working life.

Are you more than 5 years away from retirement age?

Are you are more than 5 years away from the age that you can access your retirement savings (between age 55 and 60 in Australia depending on the age you were born)?

Then the strategy is to use your employer contributions (9.25% of your salary in Australia currently) plus any extra tax incentives or employer contributions, but no more.

The rest should be invested outside of your retirement saving account as part of your Financial Freedom Strategy. I'll be covering that strategy in the next section.

If you are 5 years or less away from the age at which you can access your retirement savings, then look to maximize the use of your retirement savings account.

You will usually find that this account has benefits greater than almost any other way to invest. When you are within 5 years the major disadvantage of the funds being locked away until a certain age is reduced.

In summary, the strategy is to only contribute to your retirement account where there is a significant tax advantage to do so until you are within 5 years of retirement age, then to maximize contributions to retirement account.

Your additional savings should be used to get income producing investments outside of your retirement savings account.

These income-producing investments will add to your passive ongoing income.

This in turn will reduce the size of the retirement savings nest egg you will need to last you 25 years.

The ideal outcome to aim for however is not to need any of this nest egg for retirement income in your healthy years, but to have it aside to give you choices for the time when you unhealthy in your old age - usually around 73-75 years onwards.

This gives you choices - really important choices that you may not consider right now, such as being able to afford home help, etc.

This can allow you to live with style and grace your whole life.

Chapter 11

What you need to do

Step 1 – Who is on your team?

At this point I'd like to talk about who is on your team of 'trusted advisers'.

There is a limit to what I can cover in a book without personally working with you.

In the next two stages I'll be discussing concepts and principles in a general way.

In many cases they will be relevant to you, however it is not possible to go into details, as these very by country, and by your personal circumstances and goals. I also cannot make specific investment recommendations in a general book like this.

This is where a trusted adviser comes in. Note that I use the term 'trusted'. All of the most successful people in any walk of life surround themselves with a good team of people.

At this stage a good financial adviser and good accountant on your team are worth their weight in gold.

So the first step in going after *Financial Independence* is to have a good accountant and financial adviser on your team.

How do you find a good accountant or financial adviser? Good question.

Careful selection – be sure that they have your interests at heart, take the time to truly understand what you are trying to accomplish, and don't try to peddle you a financial product. They should be successful in their own right, and understand the principles in these books.

I usually ask this question: "What percentage of your expenses could you cover right now with the income from your investments?".

A great step can be to ask them to read this book and explain that this is the strategy that you are trying to follow. If they are overly critical of the principles or methods, I recommend that you consider walking away – there is a good chance that they will try to 'bamboozle you with bull dust'.

What I mean is that they will just try to get you to trust them without trying to educate you on exactly how their methodology will lead you to *Financial Freedom*.

At this point I hope you will indulge me if I make a plug for my team – If you would like the opportunity to work with an adviser that does understand these principles, I encourage to visit www.WealthToday.com.au (Australia only at this stage). Request to be contacted and I will refer you to one of my team.

Who is your trusted Financial Adviser?_____

Who is your trusted Accountant? _____

Step 2 - How much should you be contributing to Retirement savings?

As covered previously, it is generally accepted that you need to be putting away around 20% or more of your before tax income to have a serious chance of being Financially Independent in retirement.

This is absolutely true! However it doesn't mean that all of that money should be automatically put into your retirement savings account.

If you are more than 5 years away from retirement age, my rough rule of thumb is that a happy balance is to be contributing around 10% of your before tax income into your retirement account, and the remainder (10% plus) is used to get income-producing assets that you own outside of your retirement account.

That is quite a general rule that doesn't automatically apply to your circumstances, although it does provide a starting point.

So how much should *you* consider putting into your Retirement savings account?

It depends on the following factors:

1. Are you planning on working full-time until retirement age?

2. Is your employer currently contributing to your retirement account on your behalf? If so, how much?

3. Does your employer offer any incentives if you contribute more?

4. Does the government offer any incentives if you contribute more?

5. Are there tax incentives to contribute to your spouse or partners Retirement account?

6. Are you less than 5 years away from retirement?

Let's consider them in order.

1. Are you planning on working full-time until retirement age?

If you remember from earlier in the book we covered how to allocate your *Pay Yourself First* amount.

The basic principle is to put one-third towards saving / investing and two-thirds into debt termination.

This principle still holds true, as generally your surplus cash flow will dramatically increase once you are out of debt.

If you are planning on working full-time until retirement age, then take advantage of any incentives offered to increase your contributions to your retirement account with the one-third that you are allocating to savings / investing (once your 3 month minimum cash buffer is in place of course).

If you are seriously wishing to cut-back or stop work before retirement age then the priority changes.

Remember that generally you cannot access funds in your retirement account until you reach a certain age.

Therefore if you are wanting to stop or reduce work at an earlier age you will need to be building investments outside of your retirement account as a higher priority.

Are you planning to cut-back or stop work before retirement age? Yes / No

2. Is your employer currently contributing to your retirement account on your behalf? If so, how much?

Are you employed?

If so in many countries it is mandatory that your employer make contributions into a retirement account on your behalf. For example currently in Australia your employer must make contributions of 9.25% of your before-tax income into superannuation (Australian retirement account). This amount counts towards the suggested contributions.

In this case you could decide not to add any more over and above this, and instead focus your *Pay Yourself First* amount entirely towards debt reduction and building income-producing assets outside of retirement savings.

If you are self-employed the only person who can make contributions towards your retirement savings is you.

If you do nothing to add to your retirement savings account there will be nothing there when you need it. Unless you are really serious about stopping work early, you should be contributing to your retirement account yourself.

A good starting point is 10% of your before-tax income. Remember that it is also likely that you will get a tax-deduction for these contributions up to a certain yearly limit (check the details of this with your accountant or financial adviser).

Does your employer make retirement contributions on your behalf? Yes / No

If so, how much? _____

Do you need to make extra contributions yourself? Yes / No

How much extra will you make? _____

3. Does your employer offer any incentives if you contribute more?

For some people, their company may offer an incentive to help them build their retirement savings, for example they may match extra contributions are made up to a certain limit (e.g. if you make an extra contribution of $1000 over the year, they may match it with an additional $1000).

This can be a very effective way of boosting your retirement nest egg, and you would do well to think long and hard about taking advantage of this.

Does your employer offer any incentives to boost your retirement savings? Yes / No

If so, what is the incentive?
_____

4. Does the government offer any incentives if you contribute more?

This is very similar to the point above.

Some people may qualify for government incentives to help them build their retirement savings, for example they may give a money boost to your retirement account if you make a minimum extra contribution to your retirement account (e.g. if you make an extra contribution of at least $1000 over the year, you may qualify for a government payment of an additional $500).

This can be a very effective way of boosting your retirement nest egg, and you would do well to think long and hard about taking advantage of this.

Does the government offer any incentives to boost your retirement savings? Yes / No

If so, what is the incentive?
_____

Do you potentially qualify for this incentive? Yes / No

Are you going to take advantage of it? Yes / No

5. Are there tax incentives to contribute to your spouse or partners Retirement account?

This is also similar to the point above.

In some circumstances you may find that the government will give you tax incentives if you make extra contributions to your partner or spouse's retirement account.

Does the government offer any incentives to help boost your partner's retirement savings? Yes / No

If so, what is the incentive?
_____

Do you potentially qualify for this incentive? Yes / No

Are you going to take advantage of it? Yes / No

6. Are you less than 5 years away from retirement age?

If you less than 5 years away age it may be very sensible to maximize your contributions to your Retirement account.

As I've previously discussed, you will often the best incentives with the least tax payable when investing within a retirement account.

However the down side when you are far away from retirement age is that your money is locked away, and that the government may change the rules on you before you can access the money.

When you are closer to retirement age these risks reduce significantly, making it a potentially better strategy to focus on rapidly increasing the size of your retirement account.

Are you less than 5 years away from retirement age? Yes / No

If yes, what is the maximum amount you can contribute to your retirement account each year? $_____

How much are you going to contribute? $_____

Step 3 - Save money – Consolidate multiple accounts.

Do you have more than one retirement account?

If you have worked with multiple employers you may have more than one retirement account. If so you are probably wasting money paying multiple fees within the account.

In most cases you would be better off rolling all your various retirement accounts into just one account.

Have a chat with your financial adviser about which of your existing retirement account is the most suitable for you to roll all the others into (or if they know of a more appropriate one for you).

Do you have multiple retirement accounts? Yes / No

If yes, look to consolidate them into just one account.

Step 4 – Maximize the power of Compound interest.

Do you remember the Albert Einstein quote about Compound interest being the most powerful force in the universe? Well in this step you want to make sure that this is working for you.

You want your retirement account to grow over time.

You want the money in your retirement account to be working hard to grow, and you may have a couple of decades for it to grow until you reach retirement age and are able to access it.

The key in this step is to have it growing for you at as fast a rate as you feel comfortable.

Without going into too much detail, you will be significantly better off over time if your money is growing at 8% per year than say 5%.

With enough time on your side history tells us that this is certainly achievable. The key is not being too conservative when you still have many years until retirement age.

Getting this part right is ideally a conversation with your financial adviser. They will look at something called your 'risk profile'. This is a questionnaire that helps determine what level of 'risk' you are comfortable with trading off to achieve slightly higher long-term returns on your investments.

They will then help you select the right fund or combination of funds and other investments to maximize the power of compound interest working for you.

Have you got your retirement funds working hard for you? Yes / No

If not, it is important to review this sooner rather than later. This gives more time for your retirement nest egg to grow to a healthy size before you need it.

Chapter 12

Graduating to the next stage

So how do you graduate from Stage Three?

So how do you graduate from Stage Three and feel confident that you are *Financially Independent*?

Stage Three is about the having the comfort of knowing that you will have enough money to look after your needs for at least 25 years from the time you reach retirement age.

With this in mind there are 2 graduation points to *Financial Independence*, a Provisional Graduation and a Final Graduation.

This difference depends on how far away you are from retirement age. Quite obviously building 25 years of retirement nest egg takes time, in fact many years for most people.

The main goal is to be *Financially Free* (covered in the next stage). If you have to wait until your retirement nest egg is completely build before you go after Financial Freedom, you will probably never make it.

So I break up graduation in the following way:

Provisional Graduation – this is where you have completed and are auctioning the right steps that will see your retirement nest egg build over time.

Final Graduation – this is where your nest egg is now actually big enough to support you for at least 25 years.

So let's look at what you need to have done to graduate:

1. Provisional Graduation

Provisional Graduation is measured by achieving the following outcomes (in addition to graduating through the Financially Fit and Secure Stages 1 & 2):

1. You have a trusted financial adviser and accountant on your team.

2. You are investing 10% or more of your Total Income into your Retirement account (including the contributions that your employer makes on your behalf).

3. You are investing a minimum of 20% of your Total income overall into both your Retirement account and investments outside of your retirement account (including the contributions that your employer makes on your behalf).

4. You have a plan in action to take advantage of any employer and government incentives that can help you boost your or your partner's retirement nest egg.

5. You are at least 5 years away from retirement age.

2. Final Graduation

You graduate to Financial Independence by achieving the following outcomes:

1. Your retirement account nest egg is large enough to last until at least 90 years of age if you stopped working today (or a minimum of 25 years from retirement age).

2. Your Pay Yourself First (PYF) Account balance is above 24 months of minimum monthly expenses (note that over time it is important that

this increases steadily from the minimum of 3 months emergency cash).

3. You are debt-free (including any mortgage on your family home).

When you have accomplished the above goals, big congratulations you are now *Financially Independent,* and just one step away from complete *Financial Freedom.*

Stage Four

Your Journey to *Financial Freedom* and Beyond

Chapter 13

What you need to know

This is the stage where all the magic happens!

What do I mean by that?

If you understand this stage and get the focus and disciplines right in this area, you actually become free.

The title of this book series is 'Financially Fit', but in my experience most people are not actually interested in money at all.

What they want is to worry less about money, and to be able to enjoy life with peace of mind. You get this by focusing on freedom.

The Three Freedoms

Let me introduce you to the Three Freedoms:

1. Freedom of Money – this is having the freedom of not having to ever worry that you have enough money for how you want to live your life (I'm not talking about owning planes and the like, but having the comforts that are important to you).

2. Freedom of Time – this is having your time back under your control. To be able to spend it how and where you want without having to ask permission or justify.

3. Freedom of Place – this is being able to be and live where you want without thinking about travelling to and from your work or business.

I'd like you to think about the various worries or other stress that you have in your life right now.

Chances are that if you had the three freedoms working for you these worries would either disappear or greatly reduce.

The _key_ to having all three freedoms is *Freedom of Money* (Financial Freedom).

Financial Freedom unlocks the choice for you to have both *Freedom of Time* and *Freedom of Place*.

Having *Financial Freedom* truly changes your life. It changes everything, from how you feel when you wake up in the morning, to the quality of your relationships with your partner and your kids, through to the time you can spend with your parents as they get older,…and in particular it allows you to just enjoy and appreciate the present moment that you are in.

This is actually what this book series is about.

My mission is to help as many people as possible bring the three freedoms into their lives, by showing and helping them step-by-step how to achieve the first step – *Financial Freedom*.

Let's make sure that you are one as well.

All the prior steps have been about being prepared for this Stage.

Without acting on and graduating through the stages of Financial Fitness, Security and Independence, going for Financial Freedom can remain elusively out of reach.

In this chapter I'll be going into the key principles and concepts that you need to know in order to have the right building blocks for Financial Freedom.

In the chapter that follows I'll then show you how you put the building blocks in place, and how you check that they are working properly.

Let's talk about Assets

Let's take a look at what you own as well as what you owe, and re-evaluate what are possibly some of the most commonly held fallacies about what are actually *assets and liabilities.*

This can go a long way to understanding what you should and shouldn't be buying as assets, what types of debt are okay, and in what circumstances.

Interest

What type of interest is good interest?

The only good interest is interest that the bank *pays you*; such as on your savings and investments, *not* interest you pay the banks.

The banks will have you believe that they have a great mortgage offer for you, but the truth is that nobody wants a mortgage - any type of mortgage!

What people want is a house, not a loan.

The banks want to keep you in debt and paying them interest. Not because they are bad or immoral, but because your debts are *their* investments, and they want to keep their money out working for *them* for as long as possible.

They want to know that you can make the monthly repayments, and they have lots of tricks to keep you in debt, or get you back into debt.

Most of us are constantly bombarded with come-ons offering credit on *good or great terms:*

- Letters to raise your credit limit that only require your signature
- Ads on television
- Ads on the internet
- Radio ads
- Highway billboards
- Ads on the back of grocery receipts
- Stickers advertising low interest on cars on the floor

- And more to come as the creativity of marketers knows no bounds!

So that's their game, what should your game be?

Assets & Liabilities

What you own and what you owe, or your assets and liabilities, are of direct importance to us here.

Generally you buy things (assets) and sometimes you borrow money from the banks (debts and liabilities) to pay for them.

There are two main types of assets:

- Lifestyle assets
- Working assets

Lifestyle Assets

Lifestyle assets are things that you use for your personal needs and enjoyment.

They can save you money that you may otherwise be spending, for example on rent or on a car loan, if you own them correctly, but there are some rules to follow to be sure these do not sabotage your pursuit *Financial Freedom* goal.

While owning a car would be a *lifestyle asset,* you must also consider the any loan/s you take out to buy with these.

You should not borrow money, especially for lifestyle assets, except under very specific circumstances.

Even when buying a home you should immediately put a plan in place to repay the debt as soon as possible.

More common larger *lifestyle assets* include:

- Owning a home
- Owning a car
- And anything that is necessary to your basic lifestyle that makes more sense to own than rent

These assets are still however very expensive, not only because they take money out of your pocket every month, leaving you less to send out to earn money as investments for you (*an opportunity cost*), but they take your *after*-tax dollars out of your pocket.

Your House

"What about my house? Should I own a home? And how much should I pay for housing?"

Most people understand owning their home to be an *asset,* but remember it is a lifestyle asset. You need to live somewhere, but your own home doesn't give you cash flow.

Here are some invaluable tips on the subject of housing:

- While many banks will allow you to spending almost a third of your income on mortgage payments, *you should not spend more than 25% of your take home pay on your home.*

- If your home goes up in value over time, let this capital growth help you upgrade to your next home for free. Be very

- careful, however, that in so doing you don't sabotage your own financial plan by staying in mortgage debt for longer than necessary.
- You should plan to have paid off your home mortgage by 50 years of age at the latest. This is very important to give you the extra cash flow to invest over the remaining years to retirement age.

When saving for your first home, save the deposit, and then practice what the repayments will feel like. See what your budget is like by going through the motions before taking the dive, making sure that your budget surplus will still be healthy before you buy the property.

Working Assets

Working assets, or simply *investments*, are the assets you buy when you send your money out to work for you.

There are 3 types of working assets:

1. Cash assets
2. Income assets
3. Growth assets

These are what you want - more and more *Working Assets*.

More than that though, you want the right amounts of each of the assets, doing the right jobs.

Every asset has a specific job to do

I want you to think about any successful team.

Each member of the team has a specific job to do. This is the main thing that they must do and accomplish above all else.

If they do not do this one primary job properly they become the weak link that ends up letting the whole team down.

The coach may also have given them other secondary responsibilities, but the primary job is the absolutely vital one that must be performed to matter what.

I want you to think about your working assets in the same way.

You are the owner of the team (let's call it your *Financial Freedom Team*), your trusted advisers are the coaches, and your working assets are your players.

So what is Financial Freedom again?

Let's begin with a reminder of how I define *Financial Freedom*:

To consider yourself to be *Financially Free* you need to have your investments making enough <u>passive income</u> for you to live off without ever having to sell the actual assets.

That means that your investments are making enough money to pay for your living expenses without you ever having to work.

What do I need to know to get there?

Okay, I hope that thinking about seriously going after Financial Freedom in your life has you excited about what the possibility could mean to you.

So what do you need to know and understand? Well the first thing I'd like to cover is what you need to <u>*un-learn*</u>!

There are so many opinions, arguments and debates from so-called 'experts' in the finance field that are at best confusing, and at worst down-right deceptive about how to become 'wealthy' (it's not about becoming wealthy, it's about becoming free!).

All these opinions have one thing in common – when you look closely none of them actually _clearly_ explain how you become Financially Free.

So I'd like to spend some time first dispelling some myths.

Dispelling some 'expert' Myths.

Myth - You need to become Wealthy!

So many people talk about becoming wealthy, or if they could only be a millionaire then their life would be great.

This is a total myth!

There are many ways to be a so-called 'millionaire', and most of them do not give you the *Three Freedoms*.

This is really important.

If you seriously want to be free of money stress and have the three freedoms, then you NEED to focus on becoming *Financially Free*, not wealthy.

Freedom comes from having passive income coming into your life that you do not need to work for, not being 'Wealthy' (although when you have enough *passive income* coming in you will probably be called Wealthy as well).

Let me illustrate:

Would you rather have – Financial Freedom or Net Worth?
Would you rather have enough passive income each month that meant you never had to work again, or be called a millionaire because things you own are worth more than a million dollars (whether they actually earn you money or cost you money)?

Would you rather have Cash flow or Capital Growth?
Think about your life right now.

Would you rather have money coming into your back account each month from your investments (real cash that you can withdraw and spend as you want!), or have a statement arrive once a year saying that your 'net-worth' increased on paper?

It's completely different isn't it?

But when you talk with anyone in financial services they almost always talk about investing for growth and very seldom about investing for income.

The myth of net worth – Why it's no more than an interesting story

When people talk about net-worth or wealth, it gives you no real idea as to how free their lives are.

They may be completely financially free, or they may be very financially stressed. You actually have no idea based on their 'so-called' net worth.

Let me give you some examples:

There are 3 different people (John, Fred and Mary) who are multi-millionaires with a net worth of $3million.

John owns an expensive home worth $2million, and a holiday home worth $1million. Both of these properties cost him money in upkeep each month. John earns no investment income at all, but is a 'multi-millionaire'.

Fred owns a nice home and car worth $1million, and owns vacant land worth $2million. He earns no investment income at all from these, but is a 'multi-millionaire'.

Mary owns a nice home and car worth $1million, and owns a variety of investments worth $2million. She earns $100,000 a year in investment income at all from these, and is *Financially Free* (She only needs $70,000 a year to live on).

Oh, and Mary is also considered to be a 'multi-millionaire' (but so what?).

How would you rather be? John, Fred or Mary?

The Truth about becoming Financially Free

Invest for Income

Think about any conversation you've had with 'experts' before.

Did you ever walk away <u>clearly</u> understanding exactly what you needed to do and achieve to be *Financially Free*?

That's usually because the conversation is centered on growing your wealth or net-worth, <u>not</u> on increasing your passive or investment income.

Make no mistake – your freedom lies in you having income or cash flow regularly coming in, <u>not</u> on your net worth.

Key Principle – Focus on investing for income!

The key to becoming *Financially Free* lies in getting more and more quality assets or investments that produce regular income.

Note that I make a point of underlining the word 'quality'.

You want to be finding and buying assets that overtime are likely to increase the amount of income that they produce, rather than buying any old thing that may promise income but is unproven or unreliable.

Use Rule 3 – Reinvest your investment returns

Freedom comes over time from applying *Rule 3 – Re-invest your investment returns.*

You don't spend the income that your investments make you, but rather use the money to buy more investments that make you regular income.

Now you have the power of *Compound returns* working for you!

These new investments make more money in addition to your original investments.

Add to this your *Pay Yourself First* amount, and you are really starting to accelerate in an exponential fashion.

The more income your investments make, the more money you have to buy new investments that make you even more income.

You keep following this formula until your investments are regularly making more than your living expenses.

Now you are free!

At any point after that you can stop re-investing some or most of your investment income, stop working and enjoy your freedom! (Note that you always want to be re-investing a portion to keep some of the power of Compound returns working for you – this ultimately becomes part of the legacy that you leave behind).

Chapter 14
What you need to do

"Rather than invest for appreciation, my rich dad taught me to invest for cash flow and to treat appreciation like icing on a cake. I encourage you to do the same." ~ Robert Kiyosaki, author of Rich Dad Poor Dad

So to become *Financially Free* you need to have *passive income* greater than your monthly expenses.

To do that you need to get working assets or investments that make you income or regular cash flow passively (requiring very little or none of your time).

You need to get Income Assets!

Remember how I have said that you have to send your money out to work for you?

This money goes out and either buys or becomes different assets. Each asset is a member on your *Financial Freedom* team.

So how do you build a successful team - a team that successfully generates your *Financial Freedom*?

Well it starts with knowing what *Financial Freedom* looks like for you.

Then you (or your coaches) need to know what your team has to look like to give you that *Financial Freedom*.

After that you (or your coaches) have to find the right team members, and put them into the right positions.
Finally you (with your coaches) need check that each team member is doing their job properly and getting the expected results.

If they are not then you need to replace them until you eventually have built the correct team.

Does this make sense?

Once you have your entire team in place, and they are doing their jobs properly, then you are free!

I introduced the three types of Working Assets to you earlier – Cash, Income, and Growth Assets.

Let's now put this into a practical perspective using the principle of your *Financial Freedom Team*.

Step 1 - What much passive income do you need to be Financially Free?

Let's look at this from three different stages of life:

1. Exactly where you are right now
2. When you are debt free; and finally, if applicable,
3. When you are no longer financially supporting any kids.

1. How much *passive income* do you need to be *Financially Free* right now? (This is your Total Monthly Expenses that you worked out previously – This will give you the same lifestyle as you have right now, just not needing to work).

$_____per month

2. If you had no debts, how much *passive income* do you need to be *Financially Free*? (This is your Total Monthly Expenses minus your debt repayments).

$_____per month

3. If your kids were off your hands, how much *passive income* do you need to be *Financially Free*? (This is your Total Monthly Expenses minus your debt repayments and any expenses related to the kids).

$_____per month*

Now set the goal!

What is your target passive income number for your *Financial Freedom*?

$_____.* (let's call this your *Financial Freedom Goal* or *FFG*)

For most of you reading this your *Financial Freedom Goal* is probably close to 3 – assume you have no debts and the kids are not financially dependent on you.

Of course if you are seriously going for *Financial Freedom* while kids are still dependent on you, then you need to take this into account.

Let's look an example – John and Mary have 2 kids age 13 and 11.

Their monthly expenses are $7,000.

Of this their debt repayments make up $2,500 a month ($2,000 on the home mortgage, $400 on car repayments and $100 on credit card debt).

They have also worked out that the kids are costing them around $1,100 a month (education, sport, hobbies, food, and all the rest of those little things that keep adding up ☺).

They are hoping that the kids are financially off their hands by 21 years of age at the latest (hopefully…). This is 10 years from now.

John and Mary have set a goal to go for *Financial Freedom* and stop work by the time the youngest is 21.

Their *Financial Freedom Goal amount* is $3,400 per month.

Once they are above this amount (and debt free), they are *Financially Free*.

Step 2 – What's your *Financial Freedom Score* (or where are you at right now)?

Let's now work out how far down the *Financial Freedom* path you are right now.

I want you to add up how much passive income you currently make.

This includes such things as income the bank pays you, rent you receive from investment properties, dividend payments from shares, distributions from managed funds, profits you receive from businesses (that you do not have an active involvement in), royalty payments from books, songs, etc.

What is your <u>Total Passive Income</u> on average each month?

$_____.

If it is zero at this moment, don't get too despondent. Yes that is not a good number, but at least now you know and you can do something about it.

Now let's work out your *Financial Freedom Score (FFS)*.

Your *Financial Freedom Score* allows you to very quickly see what percentage of the way you are to reaching your *Financial Freedom Goal*.

You work it out by dividing your current Total Passive Income by your *Financial Freedom Goal* amount (FFG).

For example, using John and Mary again.

They currently get a passive income of $150 a month made up from bank interest and dividends from a small parcel of shares that they own.

John and Mary's Financial Freedom Score is:

Total Passive Income $ *150 per month* divided by

Financial Freedom Goal amount $*3,400 per month* times 100 (to give you a percentage).

Financial Freedom Score = *4.4 %* (they still have a way to go to get to Financial Freedom).

Now it is your turn:

Your *Financial Freedom Score* is:

Total Passive Income $_____ divided by

Your *Financial Freedom Goal* amount $_____ times 100 (to give you a percentage).

Your *Financial Freedom Score* = _____% (the goal is to get it above 100% as soon as possible).

Step 3 – Time to go Shopping!

So at this point you know exactly how much passive income you need to be to be *Financially Free*.

Your *Financial Freedom Score* also helps you to know exactly where you are right now (you actually have a grade or percentage score of how you are tracking.

Now it is time to go shopping ☺!

No, no, not for retail therapy…shopping for *income* assets!

Now you start finding and buying assets that will be joining your *Financial Freedom Team*.

What sort of income assets should you be shopping for?

When you start shopping you will find that there are many opportunities to spend money on 'assets'.

This is where the naïve can lose money if they don't have good principles to guide them (and obviously this is where having a <u>good</u> adviser as one of your coaches is worth his/her weight in gold!).

When you start looking you will see that almost everybody will have 'opinions and advice' about what is the best investment for you. Many of these people will be so-called 'advisers' as well.

In many cases their advice is rubbish – not necessarily because the investments that they recommend are not good, but because they are not appropriate for what you are wanting to achieve – which is to get closer and closer to *Financial Freedom* with every step you take.

While I cannot be specific about exactly which assets will suit you in this book, I can, however, give you some good principles to guide your decisions.

Investment Principles

1. *Return <u>of</u> your money is more important than return <u>on</u> your money*!

This means that you want to invest warily, and in quality investments.

Before making an investment decision you want to be reasonably sure that you will be able to get your money back (at least over the medium to long term).

So don't invest in 'the latest, greatest scheme'. Better to have good investments that have stood the test of time.

2. *The higher the return the higher the risk.*
Don't go for outrageous return – you don't need to.

If someone is promising you a high return on your money there is a very good chance that you could lose all of the money you invest.

As a rule of thumb you want to go for good quality investments that have been shown to regularly earn an income of between 5% and 12% per year.

Depending on the type of investment (again I recommend getting a good financial adviser to guide you here), this can be a sustainable return for the long-term.

3. *Don't put all your eggs in one basket!*

Never put all your money into just one investment (you may start with only one in the beginning, but make sure you spread you money into a range of different investments).

There are at least two very good reasons for this.

Firstly it is just too risky – if anything ever happens to that one investment it could have a dramatic effect on your *Financial Freedom* plans.

Secondly, no one investment will ever perform well all of the time.

Think of it like a sports team.

Your team needs to be able to play well all year round. You need a variety of team members to be able to do this effectively. Some of your team needs to be good in summer, some in winter, some in autumn, and some in spring.

As far as investment goes, what I specifically mean is that you shouldn't own just one property or just one share.

You also shouldn't just only own properties, or only own shares.

No matter what types of investments you prefer or feel most comfortable with, you should own a variety of others.

In investment circles this is known as 'diversifying' or spreading your risk.

This is a very important investment principle!

4. *Invest in quality.*
Look to buy quality investments.

This means investments that are likely to keep growing and keep earning higher amounts of income over the long term.

For properties, this means properties in areas of demand, where the demand is likely to increase over the long term (because more and more people are likely to be wanting to live in the area where the property is, and also want to live in that type of property (e.g. an apartment or a house).

For shares this means good, well known publicly listed companies that produce products or services that are always in demand. You also want them to have a track record of consistently increasing their earnings and paying regular dividends.

5. *If you can't understand the investment don't invest in it.*

My older brother (who was able to achieve Financial Freedom himself at the ripe old age of 40 years old) has a simple investment philosophy.

If he can't understand an investment he won't invest in it.

He explains this to any adviser trying to 'sell' him an investment opportunity.

He figures that if the adviser cannot explain in a simple enough fashion for him to understand and evaluate how this asset will fit into his *Financial Freedom Team,* then the investment adviser themselves doesn't really understand the investment – either way he will not invest even $1 in the investment.

This point of view is a good one to adopt.

Don't let any 'expert' try to convince you that you should just trust them if you do not understand how and where they are recommending you invest your money.

Exactly how do you invest?

Remember that at this stage you should have your *Pay Yourself First* money automatically going into your *Pay Yourself First Account* every month.

You should always keep a minimum of 3 months of your monthly expenses in your *PYF* account at all times.

The money over and above this amount is what you invest.

Where do you get started?

I have found that the key is to build your knowledge, experience and results up over time.

If you only have a relatively small amount to start with it is probably a good idea to start with a managed fund (e.g. at the time of writing this book, amounts under $100,000 are considered quite small. This is because it can be quite difficult to break it up to spread into multiple investments cost effectively under this amount).

Again remember my guidelines above.

You do not want a managed fund that only invests in one thing, or one type of asset.

Ideally you want look for one that is a 'multi-manager' (invests in multiple funds), with a focus on generating income.

This is an easy, stress-free way on concentrating on building up your income assets.

Once you're working assets are over $100,000 you then have a large enough sum consider investing in more direct assets if and when it makes sense.

Step 4 – Re-invest the income your investments make.

Remember Rule 3 –'Re-invest your Investment Returns'?

Your *Financial Freedom Team* of your income assets should be making you regular income.

Make sure that this income is being deposited directly into your *Pay Yourself First* account. Once every 3 months or so, use this money to go shopping again for more income assets.

When you do this combined with your automatic *Pay Yourself First* savings amounts that are also regularly going into you *PYF account* can you see how this will start compounding upon itself and accelerate you towards *Financial Freedom*?

Step 5 – Review and check

Now you are steadily moving toward Financial Freedom.

Keep this up and your goal is all but certain (given enough time).

Now you need to keep an eye on your *Financial Freedom Team* of income assets, check that they are doing the right jobs, and check how you are progressing.

What do you need to keep an eye on?

a. <u>What is your new FFS (Financial Freedom Score)?</u>
The first thing to regularly monitor is your *Financial Freedom Score*.

Ideally you want to see this steadily increase with each review.

This is a vital measure as it is the direct measure of how close you are to reaching your *Financial Freedom Goal*.

b. <u>Do you have too much of any one type of assets?</u>
The second area to regularly monitor is that you have a good spread of income assets.

Over time if not checked and adjusted you may find that you get a little too much of one type of asset, for example too much property or much shares relative to the other types of working assets that you own.

As I covered previously this may end up exposing you to too much risk if something unexpected happens to that one asset or type of asset (for example a downturn in property, or extended vacancy period).

Remember you want of variety of working assets on your *Financial Freedom Team* that are able to give you a reliable and consistent income in all conditions.

b. Are your assets doing their job?
The third part is to review how each asset is doing its job.

Remember that each asset is part of a team.

When you bought the asset you gave it a job to do. It's job is to produce passive income.

Is it doing that job?

If so, is it reaching the minimum expected performance? By this I mean how much income is it actually producing?

Is this at or above the minimum amount of income you require of it?

Remember earlier that I said that overall I expect my *Financial Freedom Team* to produce above 5% income per year. I don't expect that of each asset – For example you might be happy having a 3.5-4%

income coming from a particular property, but expect a minimum of 8% coming from certain shares.

If any asset is not meeting the minimum expected performance you need to consider if this is a temporary condition (in which case place it on performance notice), or if you can do anything to improve the performance.

If not then you need to replace the asset. It is not doing the job it was supposed to do, and you would be better off exchanging it for a new team member that will do a better job.

How often should you review?

I recommend that you conduct a review every 6 months.

At least once a year the review should be a formal written review that rechecks your goals, progress and asset performance. Any changes that you decide to make for the next 12 months should also be written down, including the results you expect from those changes.

Taking these steps ensures that you can look back at your progress, including your experience, successes and failures (or learning experiences), and step by step become better in guiding yourself towards not just Financial Freedom, but understand what you did to reach it.

This understanding, including who you become and the skills you learn is the gift that comes along with the journey.

This gift of knowledge and wisdom is what you will need to remain *Financially Free* once you have achieved it.

Step 6 – Keep going....until!

Keep going!

Maintain the momentum that you have started…keep moving forward.

You are on the right path, now look for ways to move faster, to accelerate down the path to *Financial Freedom.*

Earn more income, so that you can invest in even more income earning assets.

Save more.

The more you do now, the faster you will reach Financial Freedom.

How much do you want to enjoy your current life versus going for the peace of mind that comes with achieving *Financial Freedom*?

You are in the driver's seat – you decide how fast you want to go.

Chapter 15

Graduating to the next stage

So how do you graduate to Financial Freedom?

How do you know when you are *Financially Free?*

Financial Freedom is about not having to work for money.

You graduate to *Financial Freedom* when you have the comfort of knowing that you have enough passive income reliably coming in to cover your monthly expenses.

You measure it by achievement of the following four outcomes:

1. You have an effective safety net of Cash Assets in place

2. You have no lifestyle debt.

3. Your income assets are bringing in enough passive income to allow you to live the life you want right now.

4. Your retirement assets are large enough to cover any increased expenses that you may have in retirement years, for a minimum of 25 years.

When you have accomplished the above this you are now *Financially Free*!

Let's look at what total *Financial Freedom* looks like. This is about now just having enough passive income coming in, but also to have allowed for unexpected events, and for increasing expenses (e.g. medical and home care) as you age.

Let me relate this to how your *Financial Freedom Team* of assets will look like:

Remember that there are three main roles for your Working Assets or Investments.

1. Cash Assets – This is the money in your *Pay Yourself First Account*.

2. Income Assets – These are Assets outside of your Retirement Account whose job is to generate income. These are the assets that give you the passive income to need to become *Financially Free*.

3. Growth Assets – this relates to your retirement account (that contains the assets that will be available to you from your retirement age onwards – an vital part of reaching Financial Security).

1. Cash Assets (PYF Account)
Ultimately you want to have at least two years worth of household expenses to be available in cash savings.

Let's calculate the size your PYF Account eventually needs to get to.

This is your Total Monthly Expenses minus your debt repayments and any expenses related to the kids (This is your *Financial Freedom Goal* amount that we calculated this before in Step 1 of this chapter).

For example in John and Mary's case their Total Monthly Expenses were $3,400 per month.

Therefore the size of their PYF Account needs to be:

$ 3,400 per month times 24 months = $ 81,600

Now it's your turn:

This is your Total Monthly Expenses minus your debt repayments and any expenses related to the kids $_____ per month times 24 months = $_____ (Note: you want it to be at this size by the time you retire from work).

2. Income Assets

The success of this area is determined by how much passive income your income assets make for you.

The primary aim is to have assets / investments that make enough income to cover your monthly expenses.

When this is in place you are Financially Free…just.

Ideally you want these assets to be making you a minimum of 25% more than you need to cover you monthly expenses. This will allow for any variation in income that may occur from time to time.

For example, in John and Mary's case their *Financial Freedom Goal* amount was $3,400 per month.

To have the comfort of a buffer around their Financial Freedom, they would need to have:

$ <u>3,400</u> per month times 1.25 = $ <u>4,250</u> per month (this is 25% more that their goal amount to allow for income fluctuations).

This equals $ <u>51,000</u> per year of income.

Now it's your turn:

What is your *Financial Freedom Goal* amount? $ _____ per month

Multiply it by 1.25 = $ _____ per month (this is 25% more that your goal amount to allow for income fluctuations).

Multiply it by 12 = $ _____ per year of income.

When your income assets are producing this much income, you have a nice buffer around your *Financial Freedom*.

3. Growth Assets
If you are Truly Financially Free, this reduces in importance, as you are able to cover your monthly expenses in your retirement years from your income assets.

Growth Assets, however, have a vital role to plays.

They can cover any shortfall in income if you haven't been able to reach *Financial Freedom* before you hit retirement age.

They also serve as an important nest egg for later in your retirement years.

This nest egg can be the difference between being able to fund home help when you health is declining (and allowing you to stay in your home), or have to move to an aged-care facility. (Now I don't know about you, but I've got no interest in spending my final years on this earth in an old age home!)

Ideally you want your growth assets to be able to fund any shortfall in your monthly expenses for a minimum of 25 years (through to at least 90 years of age).

As I've previously stated, if you are more than 5 years away from retirement, be sure that you take advantage of any tax deductions that encourage you to contribute to your retirement account.

Also make sure that you are making regular contributions to steadily keep building the size of this nest egg.

The remainder of your focus should be on building income-generating assets.

Promises

"Your present circumstances don't determine where you can go; they merely determine where you start." ~ Nido Qubein

Have I delivered on My Promise to You?

At the beginning of this book I made you a promise.

I promised that by the end of this book you would be able to see a clear path from where you are today through to achieving *Financial Freedom*.

I promised that you would also be able to convert it into a step-by-step financial plan, and know exactly where you need to start today.

I promised that it wouldn't be easy. Like any fitness plan you should expect some degree of discomfort and discipline until the workouts become a habit.

I promised that the plan would be simple, and that it works.

I believe that I have delivered on my promise to you. Within this series of books I have given you the essence of over twenty years of my knowledge and experience.

This information is priceless!

If you are prepared to pay the price of the discipline to put the plan into action for yourself, you will become progressively financially fitter and healthier with each passing day, and eventually reach true *Financial Freedom*.

With true *Financial Freedom* comes the key to unlocking true freedom and peace-of-mind.

To put it simply, if you take the time to learn to apply these lessons in your own life, you can have a happier and more fulfilling life.

Follow the Plan.

Don't miss a step.

Have the patience and discipline to apply work through and apply each step in order.

I know the temptation can be high to just take and apply one lesson, but know that they have been shared with you in a particular order for a reason.

Follow the lessons in order, and follow each and every one of them if you seriously want to go after *Financial Freedom*.

If you take the time to do so you will begin by putting a comfortable plan in place to *paying yourself first* - automatically, each and every month.

You will be comfortably *living within your means.*

Most people find that they adjust to the new spending limits in a matter of just one or two months, but the *peace of mind* that comes from knowing that you are following a solid plan more than makes up for the early discipline you need to stick to your self-imposed spending limits.

You will make sure that you have the right *safety net* in place to protect you and your family along the way.

Over time you will begin to notice that you have *fewer debts* and are becoming a little wealthier each month.

Given enough time and saving the right amount, you will eventually build a financial wall around you and your family that is virtually impenetrable.

You will develop a *Financial Freedom Team* of assets that are paying you and even increasing amount of *passive income.*

One day you will wake up to realize that *you have done it!*

You are actually *Financially Free.*

Your time is fully back under your control and you answer to no one but yourself!

What will you do with your Freedom?

What will you do now?

How will you leave your mark on the world?

While these books are about money, in reality they are quite the opposite.

They are about getting money worries and stress out of your life. They are about helping you find your freedom, so you can pursue your passion and purpose.

If you follow the steps I have laid out for you in this book series you will become financially stronger with each passing month.

The stronger you become financially, the less important money will seem to you. You will feel the money stress melt away. And with that you will find peace of mind.

Things that once bothered you and sucked up your time and energy will become virtually irrelevant. You will find that you have the time and energy to devote to your passions.

These are what are truly important to you – these are your gifts.

I believe that each of us is meant to find our personal passion and purpose.

My passion is to help lead people to a life of freedom. Money in itself holds very little interest to me. I love to teach people how they can release the shackles of being trapped by debt, or having to work in a job or business that they are not passionate about. Helping someone find freedom that comes with moving past these areas is where my passion lies.

You now have a clean canvas to paint on with passion!

What will you do with this gift?

Now it's up to you.

'Journey of a thousand miles begins with a single step' – Lao Tzu

As you start down your path, I'd like to share some closing thoughts to help you along the way.

1. 'Happiness is a decision, not a destination!'

You can find happiness wherever you are.

Make a decision to enjoy life while you strive for your goals. It's the only life we have, so try to always look for the good and the joy in all that you do and experience. It is there...but sometimes you need to look a little harder for it.

2. Celebrate your successes along the way.

Reaching Financial Freedom doesn't happen overnight.

Set smaller goals, and celebrate when you hit them. This is great for the soul! Not only does it show that you are getting closer and closer, but it helps make the journey enjoyable.

3. Keep a journal.

Take the time to document your journey. You can include such things as challenges faced and how you overcame them, thoughts and learning's along the way, how you celebrated the achievement of milestones, etc.

This is a great way to be able to look back for inspiration in moments of discouragement or self-doubt, but ultimately it also becomes a record that you can pass down to your family so that they can have some insight to what you had to do and overcome on your journey to financial success.

4. Make a goals board.

Take or cut out pictures that help you to visualize the freedom that you are going for. Also capture how you will celebrate the successful achievement of your next milestone on your journey.

Place it somewhere prominent, for example on the kitchen fridge, where it can help remind and inspire you to stick to your disciplines and keep moving forward.

> *"It was the best of times, it was the worst of times"* – Charles Dickens
> *'A Tale of Two Cities'*

When you look back you will realize that these are the best of times and the worst of times.

The worst of times through the struggle of changing old habits, discipline and self-doubt; but the best of times through who you become, the skills you learn and the knowledge and confidence that you will be able to pass down through the generations.

The journey you are embarking on will change your family forever.

I've delivered on my promise to you. Now it's up to you to deliver on your promises to yourself.

It's time for you embrace what I have shared; apply it in your life and *'Choose Freedom'*.

To your success! - Dr Tony

Epilogue

What if I need more help?

One question that I get a lot is where can you go if you have more questions, or need more help.

In this book series I have tried my best to give you clear strategies and solutions that can help you on the path the financial freedom, but obviously there is only so far that I can go without giving advice that is personal and tailored to you and your specific circumstances.

There are 3 ways you can get more help:

1. Join our Facebook community
Over 10,000 people are already a part of our Facebook community.

If you are not already a part of it, I encourage you to join to receive daily financial tips and inspiration. You can also post questions and messages.

Join our Facebook community here: www.facebook.com/finfitwithdrtony .

2. Attend an Event

I regularly run events both live and online. They include on both live events in person, as well as online webinars and Google 'hangouts'.

In these events your able to ask the questions you want, and I can expand and go into a lot more detail on the principles, strategies and 'how-to's' that are covered in this book series.

You can find out when and where my next events are under 'events' on the Facebook page at www.facebook.com/finfitwithdrtony .

3. Choose us as your Trusted Advisers

If you like and believe in the principles and strategies covered in these books, I would love to invite you to become a client of ours.

Through my company, Wealth Today, I have put together a team of great people that are able to work one-on-one with you to ensure you get the best results.

If you would like a trusted adviser by your side to help you tailor and personalize these principles and steps for yourself, then contact me at www.WealthToday.com.au (fill in a Contact Us form).

I need your help!

We have a huge job to do.

Millions of people are living lives of quiet desperation trapped by the money stress they find themselves under. They may be members of your family, your friends, and people living in your street or neighborhood.

My mission is to help guide them out of money stress and to their own financial freedom.

I invite you to join me.

How can you help?

There are several ways you can help.

1. <u>Start with yourself.</u>
Make sure that you following the principles that I've shared with you, and are on a personal path to Financial Freedom.

The best way to help out is by being an example yourself.

2. <u>Pay it Forward.</u>
Don't keep what you learn to yourself. Pay it forward. This knowledge needs to be shared and taught to everyone.

Begin with your family and your children, then your friends and then your community.

Share this book series with those you know will benefit.

Consider starting a start a Financial Freedom support group with some friends to help support each other putting these principles into action.

Bring people to events in your area (you are also welcome to put your name down to help out at the events).

Refer people who may benefit by having a trusted adviser of their own.

3. <u>Join our team.</u>
Join us as a coach.

I'm always looking for good people to help me eradicate money stress and bring the gift of financial freedom around the world.

This can be a very rewarding profession both personally as well as financially if you are doing it for the right reasons.

We welcome anyone who is sincerely interested in helping others to learn and apply these principles in their own lives.

If you are inspired to share and help others, let me know. I invite you contact me at www.WealthToday.com.au (fill in a Contact Us form and write 'How do I become a coach' in the detail box).

Share your successes.

Finally please share your successes with me.

I love hearing how you have applied and made these principles work for you - this is the fuel for my soul!

Be sure to post your comments (or message me personally) on Facebook - www.facebook.com/finfitwithdrtony .

I would also really appreciate you taking a few minutes to post your comments or a brief review on my Amazon author's page.

https://www.amazon.com/author/drtonypennells

Thank you!

Research

- http://www.justlanded.com/english/USA/USA-Guide/Money/Credit-History
- http://en.wikipedia.org/wiki/Credit_score
- http://career-advice.monster.com/job-search/getting-started/bad-credit-and-your-job-search/article.aspx
- http://www.katu.com/amnw/segments/Rick-Emerson-190052541.html
- http://voices.yahoo.com/learning-let-go-financial-past-3154303.html?cat=3
- http://mindovermoneyinc.org/what-we-do/financial-change/
- http://moneybible.org/daily-thoughts/financial-change/
- http://www.thesimpledollar.com/2010/04/11/when-financial-change-is-overwhelming/
- http://www.psychologytoday.com/basics/habit-formation
- http://lifehacker.com/5926583/why-habits-arent-actually-formed-in-21-days
- https://www.amp.com.au/wps/portal/au/AMPAUGeneral3C?vigurl=%2Fvgn-ext-templating%2Fv%2Findex.jsp%3Fvgnextoid%3D4fef691878854310VgnVCM1000001903400aRCRD
- http://www.forbes.com/2009/03/24/wealth-manager-adviser-intelligent-investing-financial-planning.html

- http://money.cnn.com/magazines/moneymag/money101/lesson21/index.htm
- http://www.financialeducatorscouncil.org/financial-literacy-for-kids.html
- http://money.cnn.com/magazines/moneymag/money101/lesson12/index.htm

By the Author
Dr. Tony Pennells M.B.B.S, Dip. FS

ೊ

Books

Financially Fit - Book One: How to Cure Money Stress

Financially Fit - Book Two: 30 Days to Financial Fitness

Financially Fit - Book Three: Your Path to Financial Freedom

Connect with me!

I love getting feedback from my readers and would really appreciate you taking a few minutes to post your comments or a brief review on my Amazon page.

https://www.amazon.com/author/drtonypennells

Also come join our Facebook community here:

Facebook - www.facebook.com/finfitwithdrtony

Thank you!

www.ingramcontent.com/pod-product-compliance
Lightning Source LLC
Chambersburg PA
CBHW071911290426
44110CB00013B/1356